RICHARD ORR'S
NATURE
CROSS-SECTIONS

ILLUSTRATED BY
RICHARD ORR

WRITTEN BY
MOIRA BUTTERFIELD

Scholastic Canada Ltd.

A DORLING KINDERSLEY BOOK

Art Editor Dorian Spencer Davies
Designers Sharon Grant, Sara Hill
Senior Art Editor C. David Gillingwater
Project Editor Constance Novis
Senior Editor John C. Miles
U.S. Editor Camela Decaire
Production Louise Barratt
Consultant Simon Tonge

Published in Canada
in 1995 by Scholastic Canada Ltd.,
123 Newkirk Road, Richmond Hill
Ontario, Canada, L4C 3G5

First published in 1995
by Dorling Kindersley Limited,
9 Henrietta Street, London WC2E 8PS

Canadian Cataloguing in Publication Data

Orr, Richard
Richard Orr's nature cross-sections
Includes index.
ISBN 0-590-24633-X

1. Habitat (Ecology) – Juvenile literature.
I. Butterfield, Moira, 1961- . II. Title.
III. Title: Nature cross-sections.

QH541.14.077 1995   j574.5   C95-931059-2

Reproduced in Italy by G.R.B. Graphica, Verona
Printed in Italy by L.E.G.O.

CONTENTS

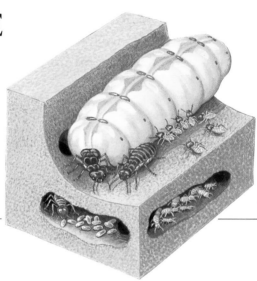
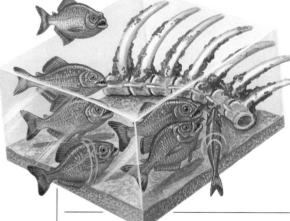

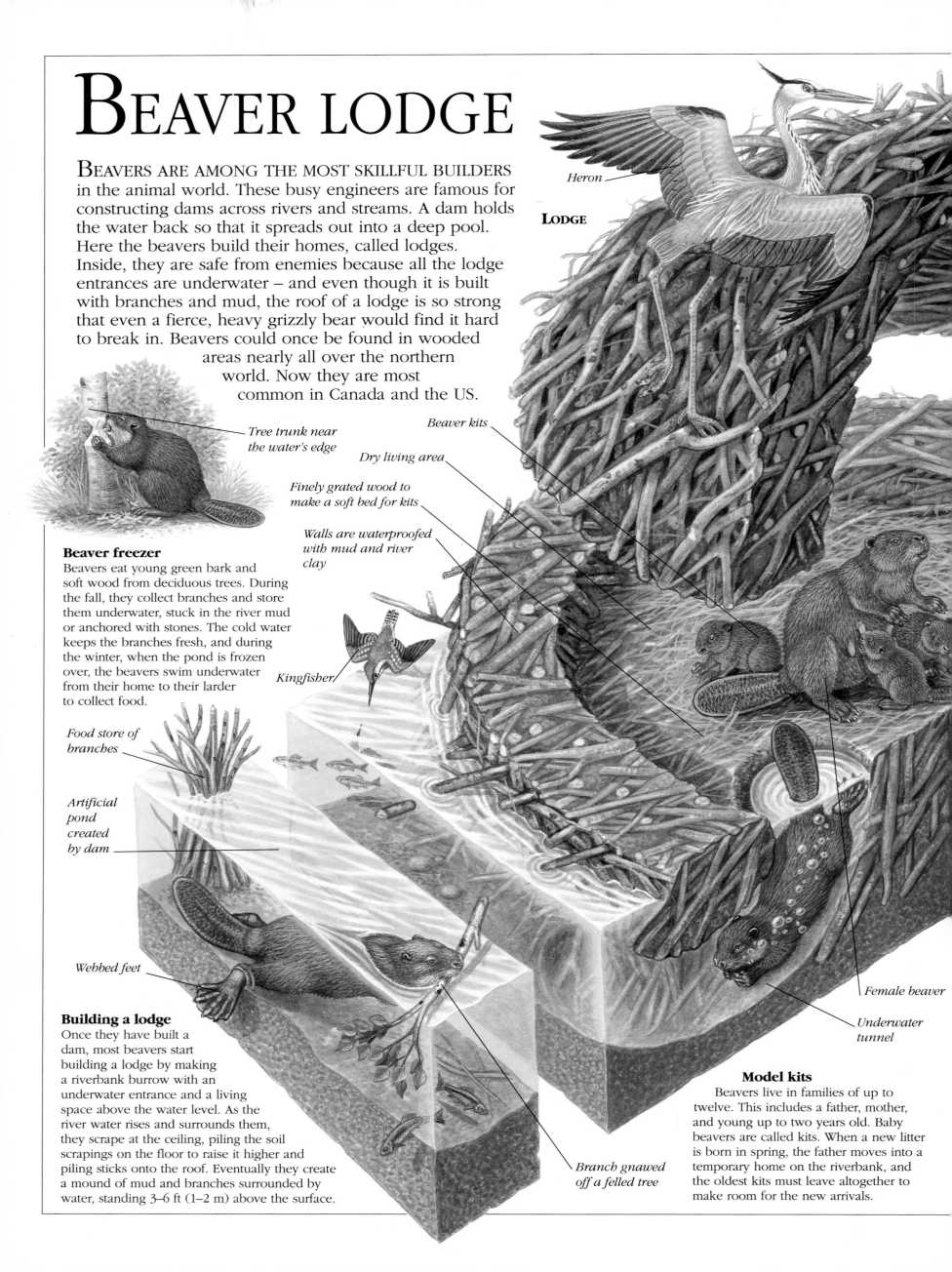

BEAVER LODGE

BEAVERS ARE AMONG THE MOST SKILLFUL BUILDERS in the animal world. These busy engineers are famous for constructing dams across rivers and streams. A dam holds the water back so that it spreads out into a deep pool. Here the beavers build their homes, called lodges. Inside, they are safe from enemies because all the lodge entrances are underwater – and even though it is built with branches and mud, the roof of a lodge is so strong that even a fierce, heavy grizzly bear would find it hard to break in. Beavers could once be found in wooded areas nearly all over the northern world. Now they are most common in Canada and the US.

Heron

LODGE

Tree trunk near the water's edge

Beaver kits

Dry living area

Finely grated wood to make a soft bed for kits

Walls are waterproofed with mud and river clay

Kingfisher

Beaver freezer
Beavers eat young green bark and soft wood from deciduous trees. During the fall, they collect branches and store them underwater, stuck in the river mud or anchored with stones. The cold water keeps the branches fresh, and during the winter, when the pond is frozen over, the beavers swim underwater from their home to their larder to collect food.

Food store of branches

Artificial pond created by dam

Webbed feet

Building a lodge
Once they have built a dam, most beavers start building a lodge by making a riverbank burrow with an underwater entrance and a living space above the water level. As the river water rises and surrounds them, they scrape at the ceiling, piling the soil scrapings on the floor to raise it higher and piling sticks onto the roof. Eventually they create a mound of mud and branches surrounded by water, standing 3–6 ft (1–2 m) above the surface.

Branch gnawed off a felled tree

Female beaver

Underwater tunnel

Model kits
Beavers live in families of up to twelve. This includes a father, mother, and young up to two years old. Baby beavers are called kits. When a new litter is born in spring, the father moves into a temporary home on the riverbank, and the oldest kits must leave altogether to make room for the new arrivals.

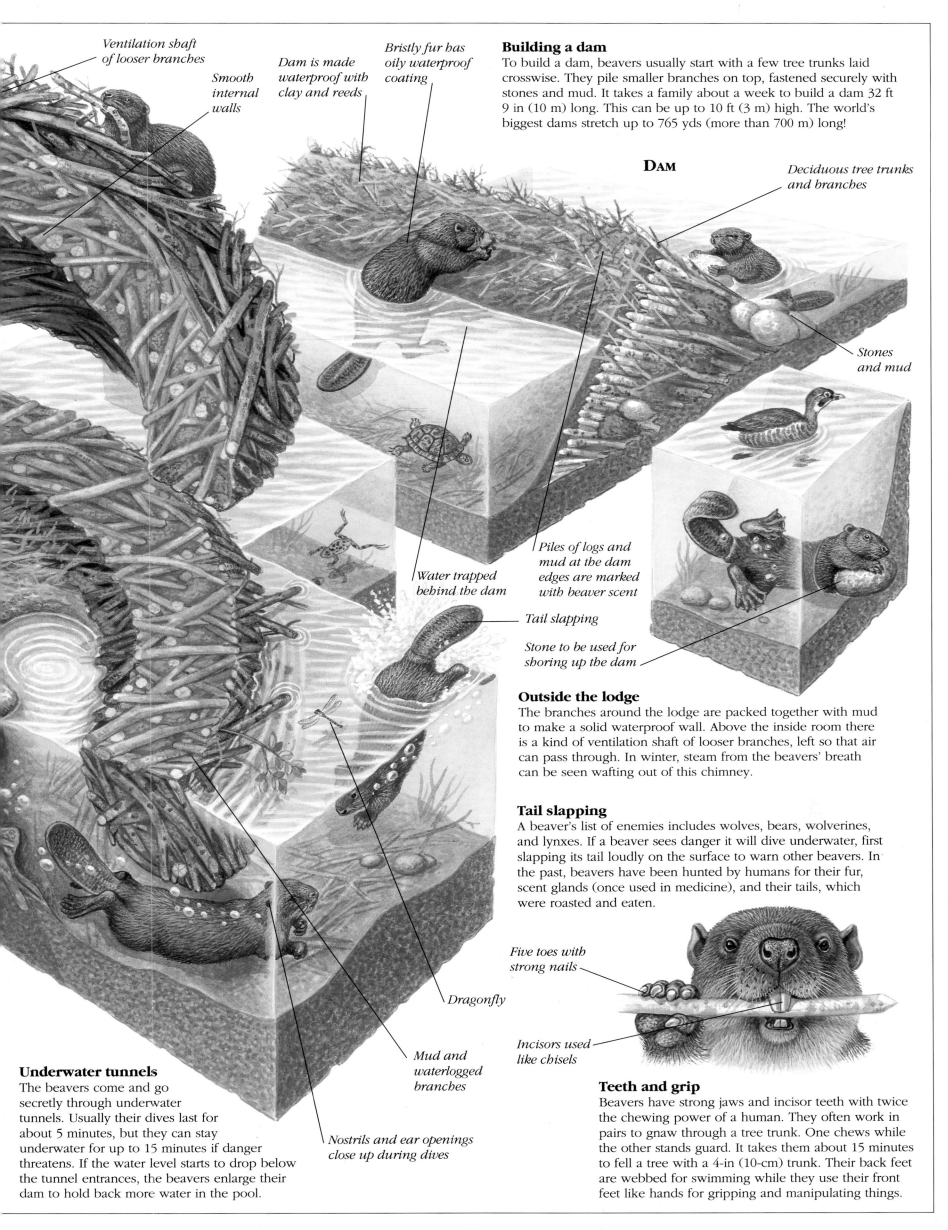

Ventilation shaft of looser branches

Smooth internal walls

Dam is made waterproof with clay and reeds

Bristly fur has oily waterproof coating

Building a dam

To build a dam, beavers usually start with a few tree trunks laid crosswise. They pile smaller branches on top, fastened securely with stones and mud. It takes a family about a week to build a dam 32 ft 9 in (10 m) long. This can be up to 10 ft (3 m) high. The world's biggest dams stretch up to 765 yds (more than 700 m) long!

DAM

Deciduous tree trunks and branches

Stones and mud

Piles of logs and mud at the dam edges are marked with beaver scent

Water trapped behind the dam

Tail slapping

Stone to be used for shoring up the dam

Outside the lodge

The branches around the lodge are packed together with mud to make a solid waterproof wall. Above the inside room there is a kind of ventilation shaft of looser branches, left so that air can pass through. In winter, steam from the beavers' breath can be seen wafting out of this chimney.

Tail slapping

A beaver's list of enemies includes wolves, bears, wolverines, and lynxes. If a beaver sees danger it will dive underwater, first slapping its tail loudly on the surface to warn other beavers. In the past, beavers have been hunted by humans for their fur, scent glands (once used in medicine), and their tails, which were roasted and eaten.

Dragonfly

Five toes with strong nails

Incisors used like chisels

Mud and waterlogged branches

Nostrils and ear openings close up during dives

Underwater tunnels

The beavers come and go secretly through underwater tunnels. Usually their dives last for about 5 minutes, but they can stay underwater for up to 15 minutes if danger threatens. If the water level starts to drop below the tunnel entrances, the beavers enlarge their dam to hold back more water in the pool.

Teeth and grip

Beavers have strong jaws and incisor teeth with twice the chewing power of a human. They often work in pairs to gnaw through a tree trunk. One chews while the other stands guard. It takes them about 15 minutes to fell a tree with a 4-in (10-cm) trunk. Their back feet are webbed for swimming while they use their front feet like hands for gripping and manipulating things.

TERMITE CITY

IMAGINE STANDING IN THE BLAZING HEAT OF AN AFRICAN afternoon. After a while it would be difficult to withstand the searing hot rays of the sun. Yet one of the most numerous creatures that lives on the grasslands of Africa, a tiny insect called a termite, has skin so soft and thin that its internal organs show through to the outside. Termites survive the sun by avoiding it, sheltering inside one of the largest and most complex animal nests in nature. From the outside it looks like a towering fortress of baked mud. Inside there is a teeming insect city with up to two million termites busy at work. Secret underground tunnels lead to the outside world.

Building the fortress
Millions of termites work together to build a nest, called a termitarium. Each creature makes its own mini-bricks by chewing earth mixed with saliva. The tiny pellets are pushed onto the wall where they dry rock-hard. The biggest nests take decades to build. The largest stretch more than 26 ft (8 m) high.

Insect air-conditioning
Termites build tiny channels through the ribs of the nest and wider chimneys up the middle. During the day, the air inside warms up and rises through the chimneys. Then it travels down through the rib channels, passing near the outer surface and getting new supplies of oxygen.

Fungus gardening
Termites eat plant material. But the fibrous part of plants, called cellulose, is very difficult to digest. Worker termites collect leaf pieces and chew them up to make compost, which they use to fill chambers in the nest. To this mixture they add the spores of a unique type of fungus. Soon this grows into a thick mesh called a comb. It turns the compost into a crumbly mixture that the termites can eat.

Lilac-breasted rollers catch flying termites

Mushroom provides spores for termites after it has withered

Four-toed hedgehog forages for a meal

Side chimney

Central chimney

Attic

Mongoose looks for insects in deserted mounds

African grassland, called savanna

Thick wall

Aardvark rips out part of nest

Strong claws for digging and ripping

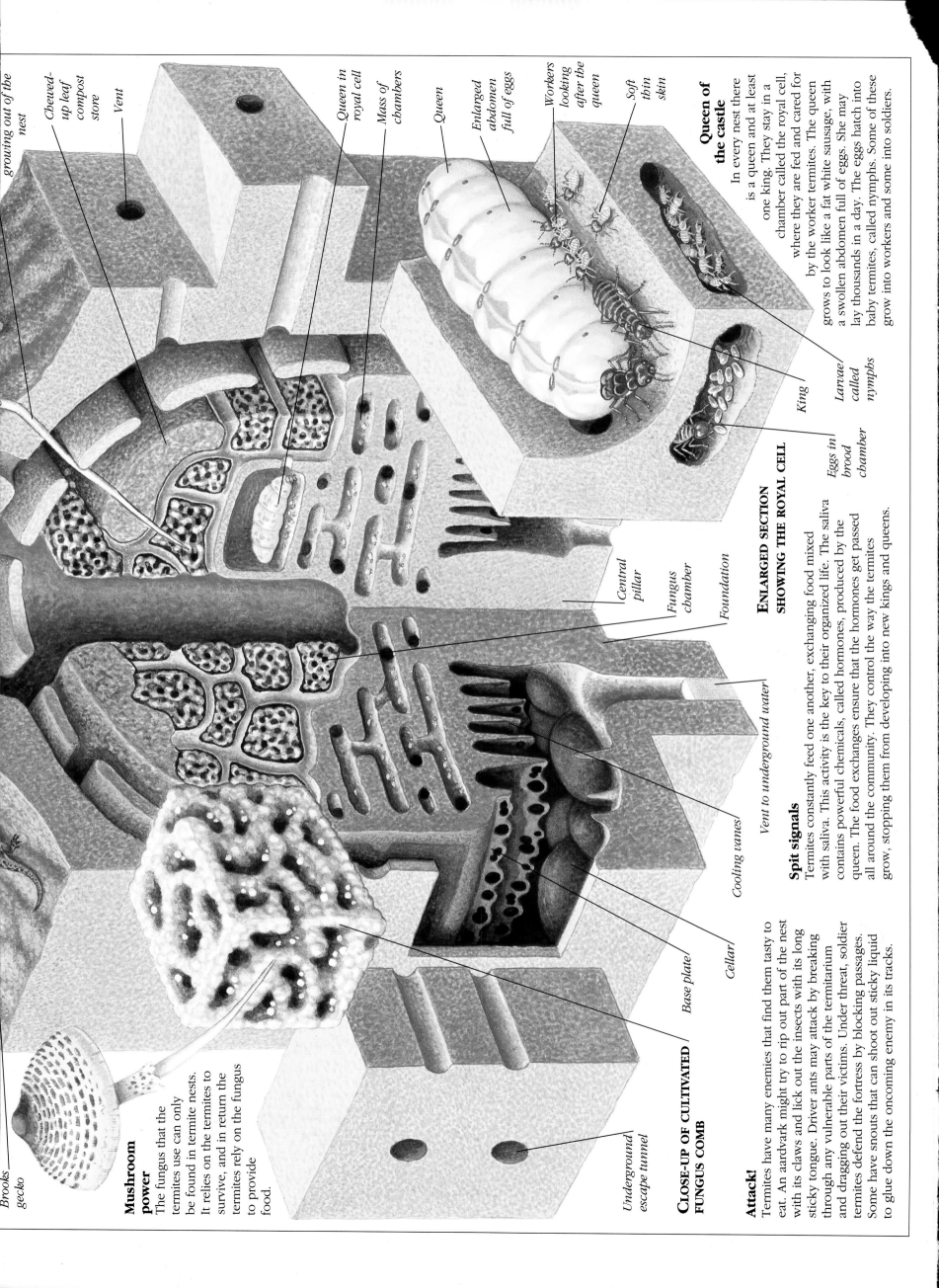

Brooks the gecko

growing out of the nest

Chewed-up leaf compost store

Vent

Queen in royal cell

Mass of chambers

Queen

Enlarged abdomen full of eggs

Workers looking after the queen

Soft thin skin

Queen of the castle

In every nest there is a queen and at least one king. They stay in a chamber called the royal cell, where they are fed and cared for by the worker termites. The queen grows to look like a fat white sausage, with a swollen abdomen full of eggs. She may lay thousands in a day. The eggs hatch into baby termites, called nymphs. Some of these grow into workers and some into soldiers.

King

Larvae called nymphs

Eggs in brood chamber

Mushroom power

The fungus that the termites use can only be found in termite nests. It relies on the termites to survive, and in return the termites rely on the fungus to provide food.

Central pillar

Fungus chamber

Foundation

ENLARGED SECTION SHOWING THE ROYAL CELL

Spit signals

Termites constantly feed one another, exchanging food mixed with saliva. This activity is the key to their organized life. The saliva contains powerful chemicals, called hormones, produced by the queen. The food exchanges ensure that the hormones get passed all around the community. They control the way the termites grow, stopping them from developing into new kings and queens.

Cooling vanes

Vent to underground water

CLOSE-UP OF CULTIVATED FUNGUS COMB

Base plate

Cellar

Attack!

Termites have many enemies that find them tasty to eat. An aardvark might try to rip out part of the nest with its claws and lick out the insects with its long sticky tongue. Driver ants may attack by breaking through any vulnerable parts of the termitarium and dragging out their victims. Under threat, soldier termites defend the fortress by blocking passages. Some have snouts that can shoot out sticky liquid to glue down the oncoming enemy in its tracks.

Underground escape tunnel

Montezuma oropendola

The crowded canopy

The majority of rain forest creatures live in the foliage 98–164 ft (30–50 m) above the ground, in the area called the canopy. It is home to countless different insects, birds, frogs, reptiles, and small mammals. It is a rich food store full of flowers, juicy fruits, and berries.

Two-toed sloth

Emerald tree boa

Fruit bat

Keel-billed toucan

Great jacamar

Kinkajou

Black spider monkey

Bromeliad

Collared trogon

CANOPY AREA - *Approx. 98–164 ft (30–50 m) high*

Quetzal

Toco toucan

MORPHO BUTTERFLY

Waxy waterproof spear-shaped leaves

JUNGLE ORCHID

Scarlet macaw

Chestnut woodpecker

White-beaded saki

EMPEROR TAMARIN

Potoo

Puffbird

LEAF-CUTTER ANT

Spix guan

White-faced capuchin

KATYDID

RAIN FOREST

TRY TO IMAGINE WHAT IT WOULD BE LIKE STANDING DEEP IN THE Amazon rain forest. You would be in a hot, steamy, gloomy place where the air itself is sticky with moisture. Giant trees would tower over your head, blocking out the light. Mysterious howls and screeches would come from unseen creatures high above you. If you wanted to see more of the wildlife, you would have to climb up one of the smooth tree trunks around you to a height of about 100 ft (30 m). There you would find the richest wildlife habitat anywhere in the world.

Top trees

Most of the trees grow about 164 ft (50 m) high, but a few "emergent" trees tower above the others at about 197 ft (60 m). They provide a home for one of the jungle's deadliest hunters, the harpy eagle. These giant birds of prey sit on their nest platforms watching the trees below. Occasionally they swoop down to grab monkeys and birds in their sharp talons.

Noisy nights

The rain forest is rarely quiet. Animal screeches and calls echo through the canopy, especially at night when there are more creatures on the move than ever. The loudest noises are made by howler monkeys. Their screech is amplified by a loose piece of throat skin that acts as a kind of voice box. Troops of howler monkeys often screech loudly together in the evening and at first light.

SMALLER CREATURES

ANOPHELES MOSQUITO (CARRIES MALARIA DISEASE)

RUBY-TOPAZ HUMMINGBIRD

HELICONIUS CATERPILLAR

White-collared swift

Guianan toucanet   *Harpy eagle*

Turquoise-browed motmot

Ferris and moss grow along branches

Three-wattled bellbird

Amazonian umbrella bird

Hyacinthine macaw

Blue-and-yellow macaw

Blue-fronted parrot

Squirrel monkey
Howler monkey

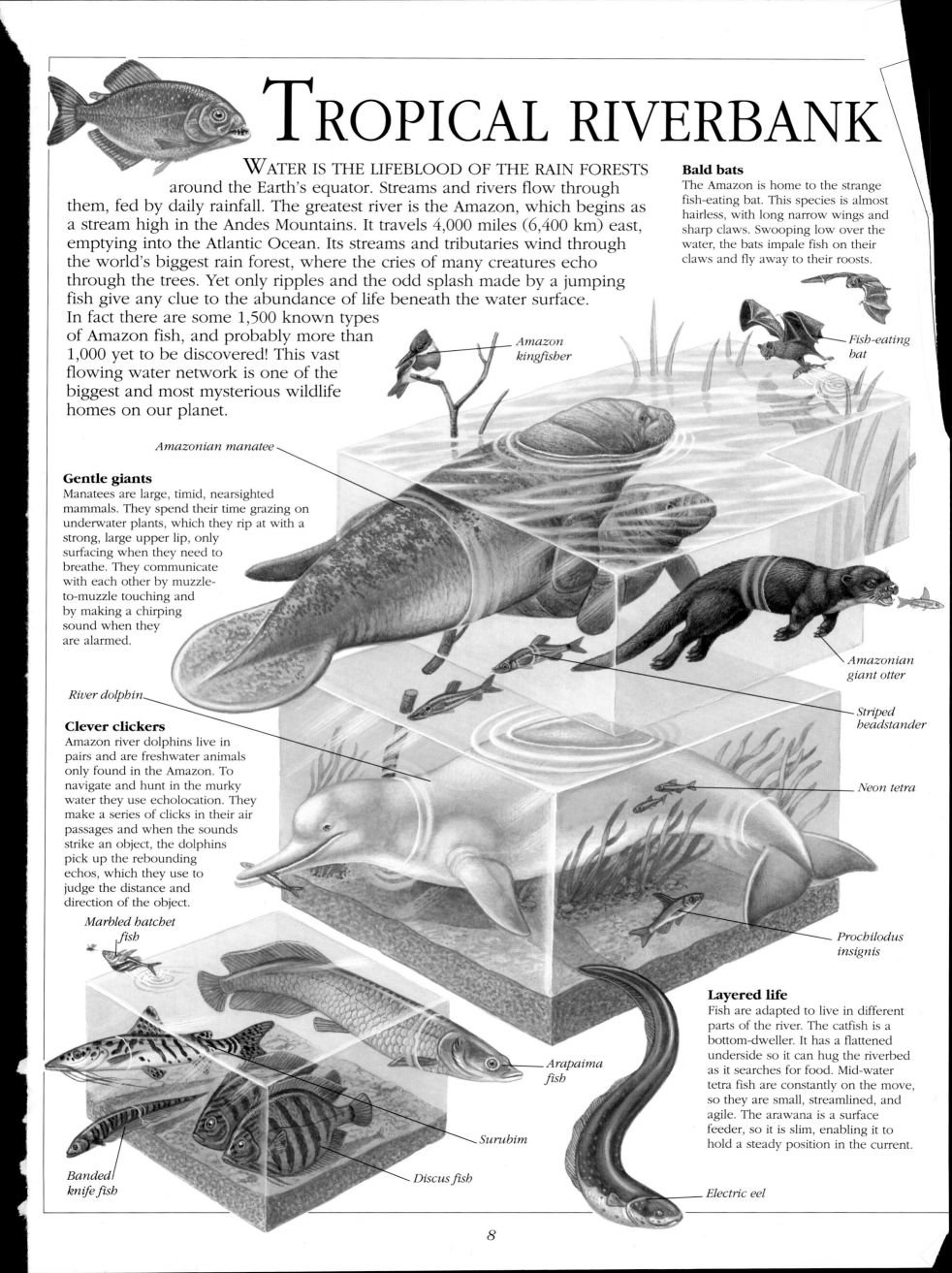

TROPICAL RIVERBANK

WATER IS THE LIFEBLOOD OF THE RAIN FORESTS around the Earth's equator. Streams and rivers flow through them, fed by daily rainfall. The greatest river is the Amazon, which begins as a stream high in the Andes Mountains. It travels 4,000 miles (6,400 km) east, emptying into the Atlantic Ocean. Its streams and tributaries wind through the world's biggest rain forest, where the cries of many creatures echo through the trees. Yet only ripples and the odd splash made by a jumping fish give any clue to the abundance of life beneath the water surface. In fact there are some 1,500 known types of Amazon fish, and probably more than 1,000 yet to be discovered! This vast flowing water network is one of the biggest and most mysterious wildlife homes on our planet.

Bald bats
The Amazon is home to the strange fish-eating bat. This species is almost hairless, with long narrow wings and sharp claws. Swooping low over the water, the bats impale fish on their claws and fly away to their roosts.

Amazon kingfisher

Fish-eating bat

Amazonian manatee

Gentle giants
Manatees are large, timid, nearsighted mammals. They spend their time grazing on underwater plants, which they rip at with a strong, large upper lip, only surfacing when they need to breathe. They communicate with each other by muzzle-to-muzzle touching and by making a chirping sound when they are alarmed.

River dolphin

Clever clickers
Amazon river dolphins live in pairs and are freshwater animals only found in the Amazon. To navigate and hunt in the murky water they use echolocation. They make a series of clicks in their air passages and when the sounds strike an object, the dolphins pick up the rebounding echos, which they use to judge the distance and direction of the object.

Amazonian giant otter

Striped headstander

Neon tetra

Prochilodus insignis

Marbled hatchet fish

Layered life
Fish are adapted to live in different parts of the river. The catfish is a bottom-dweller. It has a flattened underside so it can hug the riverbed as it searches for food. Mid-water tetra fish are constantly on the move, so they are small, streamlined, and agile. The arawana is a surface feeder, so it is slim, enabling it to hold a steady position in the current.

Arapaima fish

Surubim

Banded knife fish

Discus fish

Electric eel

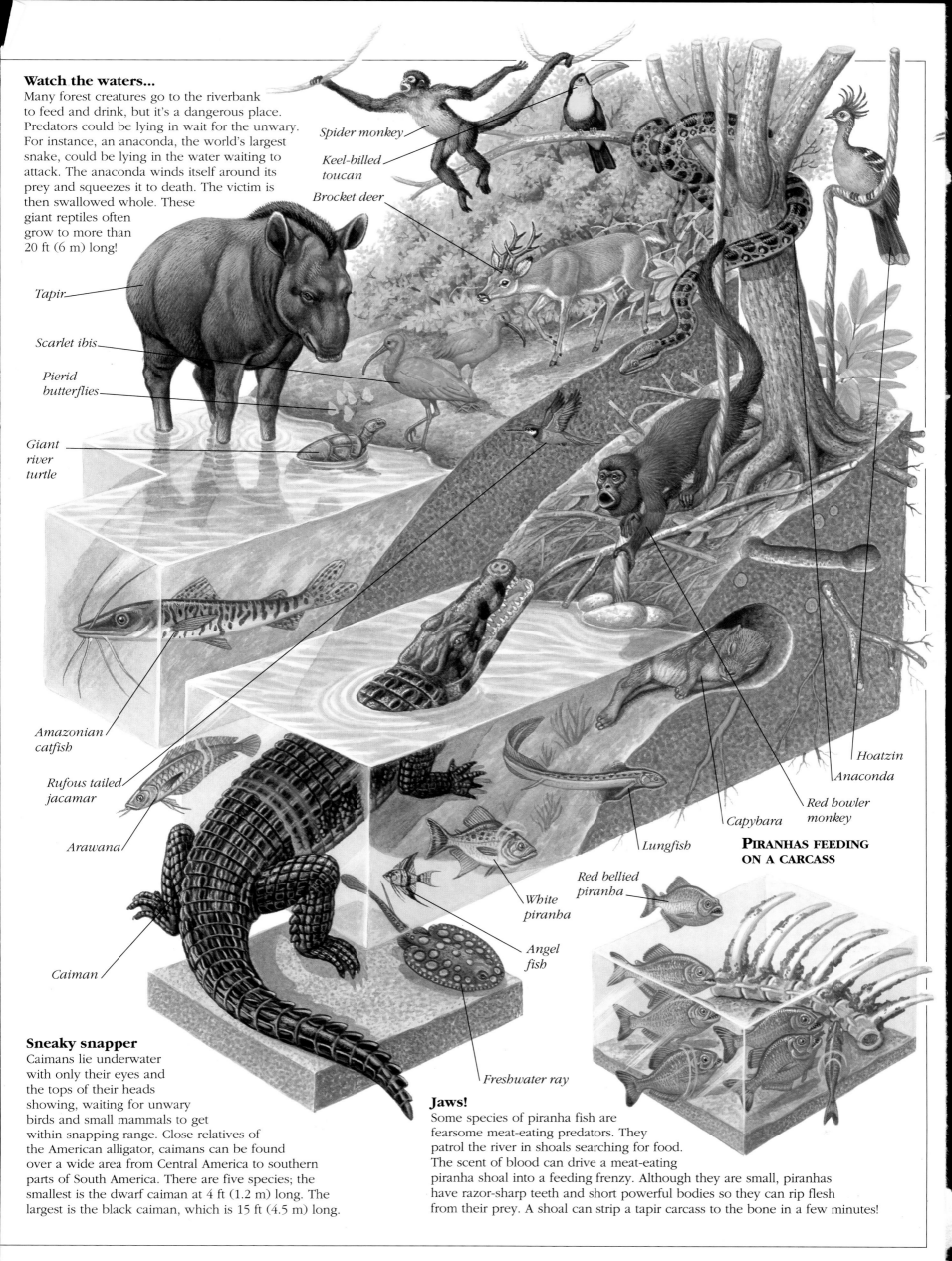

Watch the waters...

Many forest creatures go to the riverbank to feed and drink, but it's a dangerous place. Predators could be lying in wait for the unwary. For instance, an anaconda, the world's largest snake, could be lying in the water waiting to attack. The anaconda winds itself around its prey and squeezes it to death. The victim is then swallowed whole. These giant reptiles often grow to more than 20 ft (6 m) long!

Spider monkey

Keel-billed toucan

Brocket deer

Tapir

Scarlet ibis

Pierid butterflies

Giant river turtle

Amazonian catfish

Rufous tailed jacamar

Arawana

Caiman

Hoatzin

Anaconda

Red howler monkey

Capybara

Lungfish

PIRANHAS FEEDING ON A CARCASS

Red bellied piranha

White piranha

Angel fish

Freshwater ray

Sneaky snapper

Caimans lie underwater with only their eyes and the tops of their heads showing, waiting for unwary birds and small mammals to get within snapping range. Close relatives of the American alligator, caimans can be found over a wide area from Central America to southern parts of South America. There are five species; the smallest is the dwarf caiman at 4 ft (1.2 m) long. The largest is the black caiman, which is 15 ft (4.5 m) long.

Jaws!

Some species of piranha fish are fearsome meat-eating predators. They patrol the river in shoals searching for food. The scent of blood can drive a meat-eating piranha shoal into a feeding frenzy. Although they are small, piranhas have razor-sharp teeth and short powerful bodies so they can rip flesh from their prey. A shoal can strip a tapir carcass to the bone in a few minutes!

Down below
Beneath the canopy is a layer of young trees and palms. This dimly lit area is called the understory. The atmosphere is damp and airless, like a steamy bathroom.

Boat-billed heron

Three-toed sloth

Sapling tree

UNDERSTORY AREA
Approx. 17–59 ft (5–18 m) high

Buttress root - 13–16 ft (4–5 m) high and wide

Tayra

Anaconda

Small stream

Leaf litter

Coati

Paca

Scarlet ibis

Cock-of-the-rock

Smooth trunk

Ocelot

Jaguar

Toucanet

Prehensile-tailed porcupine

On the ground
The forest floor is covered with a layer of rotting plant material called leaf litter. Insects scuttle around and a few large creatures, such as tapirs, forage on the floor looking for food. Decaying plants and animal bodies release nutrients into the soil. Trees need to gather these nutrients in order to grow. Each rain forest tree grows a thick mat of rootlets just below the surface so that it can get the nutrients as quickly as possible, before the rain washes them away.

POISON ARROW FROG

NECTAR SIPPING BAT

WASP NEST

Tapir

Agoutis

RHINOCEROS BEETLE

Fungi thrive on the forest floor

Six-banded armadillo

Lots of insects live on the floor

GIANT FLATWORM

Shallow spreading rootlets

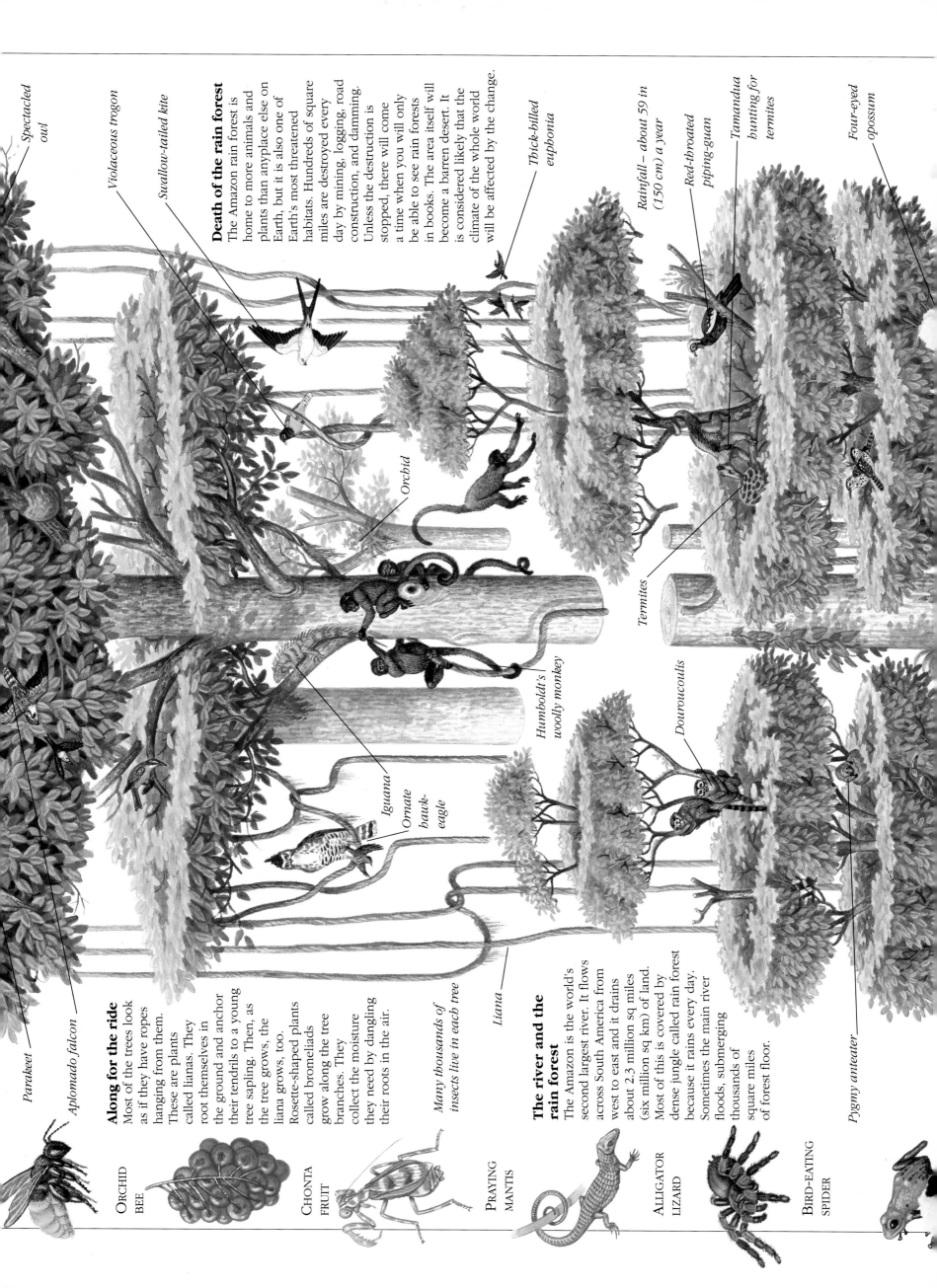

Spectacled owl

Violaceous trogon

Swallow-tailed kite

Death of the rain forest
The Amazon rain forest is home to more animals and plants than anyplace else on Earth, but it is also one of Earth's most threatened habitats. Hundreds of square miles are destroyed every day by mining, logging, road construction, and damming. Unless the destruction is stopped, there will come a time when you will only be able to see rain forests in books. The area itself will become a barren desert. It is considered likely that the climate of the whole world will be affected by the change.

Thick-billed euphonia

Rainfall – about 59 in (150 cm) a year

Red-throated piping-guan

Tamandua hunting for termites

Four-eyed opossum

Orchid

Humboldt's woolly monkey

Termites

Douroucoulis

Iguana

Ornate hawk-eagle

Parakeet

Aplomado falcon

Along for the ride
Most of the trees look as if they have ropes hanging from them. These are plants called lianas. They root themselves in the ground and anchor their tendrils to a young tree sapling. Then, as the tree grows, the liana grows, too. Rosette-shaped plants called bromeliads grow along the tree branches. They collect the moisture they need by dangling their roots in the air.

ORCHID BEE

CHONTA FRUIT

Many thousands of insects live in each tree

Liana

PRAYING MANTIS

The river and the rain forest
The Amazon is the world's second largest river. It flows across South America from west to east and it drains about 2.3 million sq miles (six million sq km) of land. Most of this is covered by dense jungle called rain forest because it rains every day. Sometimes the main river floods, submerging thousands of square miles of forest floor.

ALLIGATOR LIZARD

BIRD-EATING SPIDER

Pygmy anteater

WOODLAND

IF YOU TAKE A WALK THROUGH A FOREST IN A NORTHERN part of the world, it might seem to be a calm, peaceful place. But unseen, and perhaps very close to you, a life-and-death battle might be taking place, animals might be busy building homes and giving birth, or a stealthy hunter might be stalking its prey. Large areas of deciduous woodland flourish in North America, Europe, and central Asia, where there is mild weather and regular rainfall. Deciduous woodlands contain broad-leaved trees that drop all their leaves seasonally every winter. Oak, elm, and beech trees are all deciduous. This picture shows a European deciduous woodland – home to a large variety of plants and animals.

European brown bear

Crow

Great tit

Sparrowhawk

Fallow deer with fawn

Foxes in their burrow, called an earth

Big bears
The woodland animal that strikes most fear into humans is the bear. The European brown bear in this picture can weigh up to 550 lb (250 kg) and reach 8 ft (2.5 m) high standing on its hind legs. Although female bears can be particularly dangerous when defending their cubs, bears are normally shy creatures. In fact, they are very nearsighted. They make up for it with a sharp sense of hearing and of smell.

Mole

Bird land
Insects, nuts, seeds, and berries make the woods a rich summer feeding ground for birds. Their bodies are adapted to help them feed in different ways. Woodpeckers have stiff tails and feet with toes to help them cling to tree trunks. Their pointed beaks are good for digging into trunks, and their long tongues reach insects under the bark.

Drassodes spider

LEAF LITTER
Sexton beetle

Great brown weevil larva

Litter bugs
Insects make up 70 percent of the animal species in a woodland. Some insects live in the layer of dead leaves known as leaf litter. Together with fungi and bacteria, they break down the dead leaves. This material is then churned up by earthworms that mix the nutrients from the leaves with the soil, making it rich enough for new plants to grow in. The whole process takes about two years.

Worm cast

Centipede

Bank vole

Jay with an acorn

Earthworm

Sow bug

Wireworm

Sulphur butterfly

European hedgehog

The twilight zone
Foxes, badgers, moles, and rabbits are just some of the animals that make their homes underground. The mole is highly suited to this lifestyle. On the end of its short, wide front legs are claws that turn outward, which are ideal for digging and crawling. Because they spend most of their life in the dark, moles are very nearsighted

Bullfinch

Pine marten

Green woodpecker and young

Treecreeper

Dryad's saddle

Giant petrel

Pipistrelle bat roosting

Green woodpecker

Sulfur tuft

Honeysuckle

Fritillary

Bluebells

Cross-section through a squirrel's drey

Eagle-owl

Red squirrel

Yellow-necked field mouse

Cuckoopint

Foxglove

Wild boar

Silent swoop
Owls have specially adapted feathers that dampen the noise of their wingbeats, so they can swoop almost silently onto their prey. The eagle-owl is one of the largest owls, up to 27 in (70 cm) long with a wingspan of about 63 in (160 cm). It mainly feeds on rabbits and other birds.

Busy as a squirrel
The red squirrel spends most of its life in trees looking for nuts, seeds, buds, and insects to eat. It builds its nest, called a drey, high up in a tree using twigs and branches. Deep inside the covered nest, the squirrel's babies are safe. They need protection because they start life tiny, blind, and helpless.

Big pig
Wild boars live alone or in small groups and spend most of their time rooting for grubs, worms, seeds, and fruits. They are usually shy but can get aggressive if they feel threatened. An adult male can be particularly dangerous because it may weigh up to 441 lb (200 kg) and two of its front teeth curve up to form sharp tusks.

Giant puffball

Weasel

Stoat

Edible dormouse asleep

Parasol mushroom

Mole

Badgers in their burrow, called a sett

Hard fern

Rabbit kittens

Ring-necked pheasant

Rabbit

Woodcock

Clever colors
Animals use color to help them escape attack. Some have coats colored to blend in with the background, such as the woodcock in this picture with brown plumage the same shade as the dead leaves on the forest floor. Some woodland insects have brightly colored bodies that send a visual signal saying "I taste horrible."

The deadly chase
Forest life is an unending struggle to eat and avoid being eaten. Animals are adapted to hunt in different ways. Pine martens are agile tree climbers, which helps them hunt squirrels. Weasels and stoats have slim, wiry bodies, so they can chase animals into their underground burrows. The sparrowhawk attacks other birds in flight and will even fly into houses to get its quarry.

OAK TREE

THIS TALL, MAJESTIC OAK TREE MAY HAVE lived for up to 600 years, spreading its branches up to 100 ft (30 m) high.

Oak wood is prized for its strength and has been used for centuries to build palaces and galleons, treasure chests and thrones. Yet an oak starts life as a tiny acorn no bigger than a thumbnail, and it has to survive many dangers. Insects, birds, and squirrels eat acorns, and even if one takes root, it may still be eaten or stepped on. These mighty giants of the forest have a tough childhood!

Food-making leaves

Leaves make nutrients (the tree's food) using a green chemical called chlorophyll. In sunlight, each leaf photosynthesizes. This means that the chlorophyll traps energy from sunlight and uses it to convert minerals and water (brought up from the tree roots) and air (taken in through tiny holes called stomata in the leaves) into food.

Foliage feeders

Oak leaves provide food for insects. A big oak can support up to 400,000 caterpillars at once. It defends itself from insect attacks by quickly replacing eaten buds and producing a bitter chemical, called tannin, that repels insects.

Oak galls

Many oak trees have wartlike growths on them called galls. They are caused when insects lay their eggs somewhere on the oak and secrete substances that make tree cells grow around the eggs. This helps both the insect and the tree. The gall surrounds the larva (growing insect) so that it can't attack the rest of the tree, while the larva gets food and shelter inside the gall. Birds peck at galls to get at the larva inside.

OAK GALLS

Marble gall

Oak-apple gall

Gall wasp

Gall wasps

There are many types of galls. The oak-apple gall is one of the most common. It is caused by a wasp that lays its eggs in leaf buds in spring. The oak-apple gall grows around the eggs.

Common spangle gall

Rook

Red kite

Turtle dove

Jay

Stock dove

Redstart

Wryneck

Chaffinch

Blackcap

Golden oriole

Song thrush

Magpie

Blue tit

Pied flycatcher

TIDE POOL

IF YOU EVER GET THE CHANCE TO WALK ALONG A ROCKY SEASHORE, MAKE SURE THAT YOU look out for tide pools. They are like little oceans in miniature, providing a home for an enormous variety of different animals and plants. Life in a tide pool depends on the sea tide going in and out. When it comes in, it washes over the rocks, bringing cool, clean water. When it goes out, it leaves a pool behind, and it sometimes leaves animals stranded there.

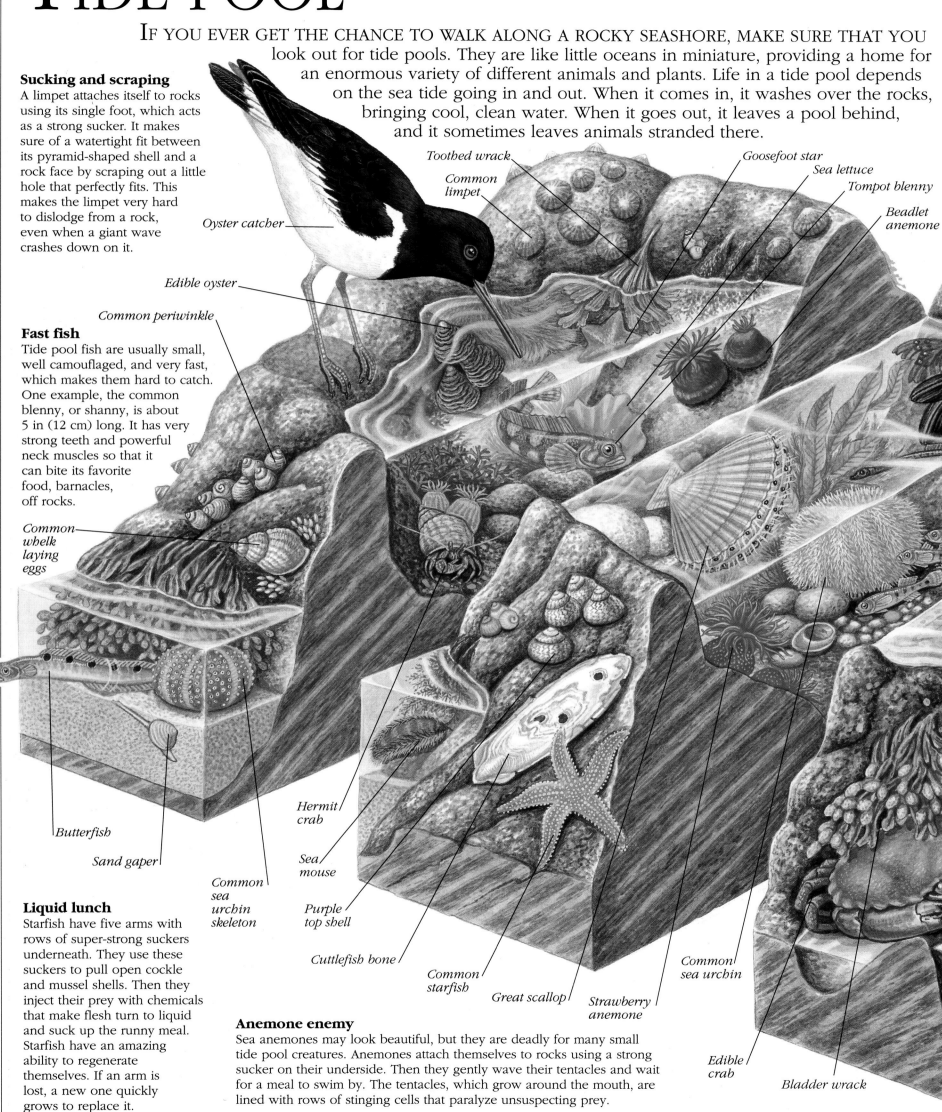

Sucking and scraping
A limpet attaches itself to rocks using its single foot, which acts as a strong sucker. It makes sure of a watertight fit between its pyramid-shaped shell and a rock face by scraping out a little hole that perfectly fits. This makes the limpet very hard to dislodge from a rock, even when a giant wave crashes down on it.

Fast fish
Tide pool fish are usually small, well camouflaged, and very fast, which makes them hard to catch. One example, the common blenny, or shanny, is about 5 in (12 cm) long. It has very strong teeth and powerful neck muscles so that it can bite its favorite food, barnacles, off rocks.

Liquid lunch
Starfish have five arms with rows of super-strong suckers underneath. They use these suckers to pull open cockle and mussel shells. Then they inject their prey with chemicals that make flesh turn to liquid and suck up the runny meal. Starfish have an amazing ability to regenerate themselves. If an arm is lost, a new one quickly grows to replace it.

Anemone enemy
Sea anemones may look beautiful, but they are deadly for many small tide pool creatures. Anemones attach themselves to rocks using a strong sucker on their underside. Then they gently wave their tentacles and wait for a meal to swim by. The tentacles, which grow around the mouth, are lined with rows of stinging cells that paralyze unsuspecting prey.

Oyster catcher

Edible oyster

Common periwinkle

Common whelk laying eggs

Butterfish

Sand gaper

Common sea urchin skeleton

Hermit crab

Sea mouse

Purple top shell

Cuttlefish bone

Common starfish

Great scallop

Strawberry anemone

Common sea urchin

Edible crab

Bladder wrack

Toothed wrack

Common limpet

Goosefoot star

Sea lettuce

Tompot blenny

Beadlet anemone

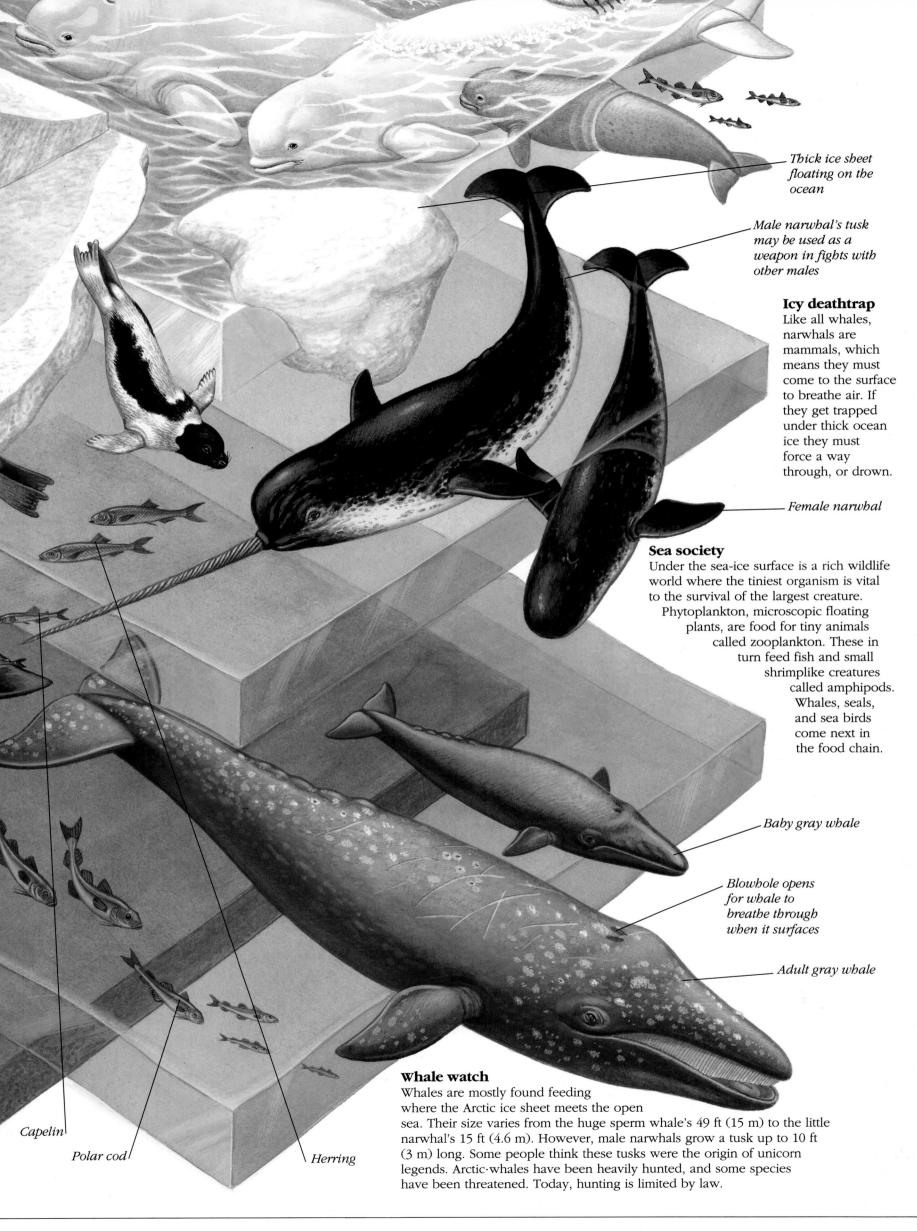

Thick ice sheet
floating on the
ocean

Male narwhal's tusk
may be used as a
weapon in fights with
other males

Icy deathtrap
Like all whales,
narwhals are
mammals, which
means they must
come to the surface
to breathe air. If
they get trapped
under thick ocean
ice they must
force a way
through, or drown.

Female narwhal

Sea society
Under the sea-ice surface is a rich wildlife
world where the tiniest organism is vital
to the survival of the largest creature.
Phytoplankton, microscopic floating
plants, are food for tiny animals
called zooplankton. These in
turn feed fish and small
shrimplike creatures
called amphipods.
Whales, seals,
and sea birds
come next in
the food chain.

Baby gray whale

Blowhole opens
for whale to
breathe through
when it surfaces

Adult gray whale

Capelin

Polar cod

Herring

Whale watch
Whales are mostly found feeding
where the Arctic ice sheet meets the open
sea. Their size varies from the huge sperm whale's 49 ft (15 m) to the little
narwhal's 15 ft (4.6 m). However, male narwhals grow a tusk up to 10 ft
(3 m) long. Some people think these tusks were the origin of unicorn
legends. Arctic·whales have been heavily hunted, and some species
have been threatened. Today, hunting is limited by law.

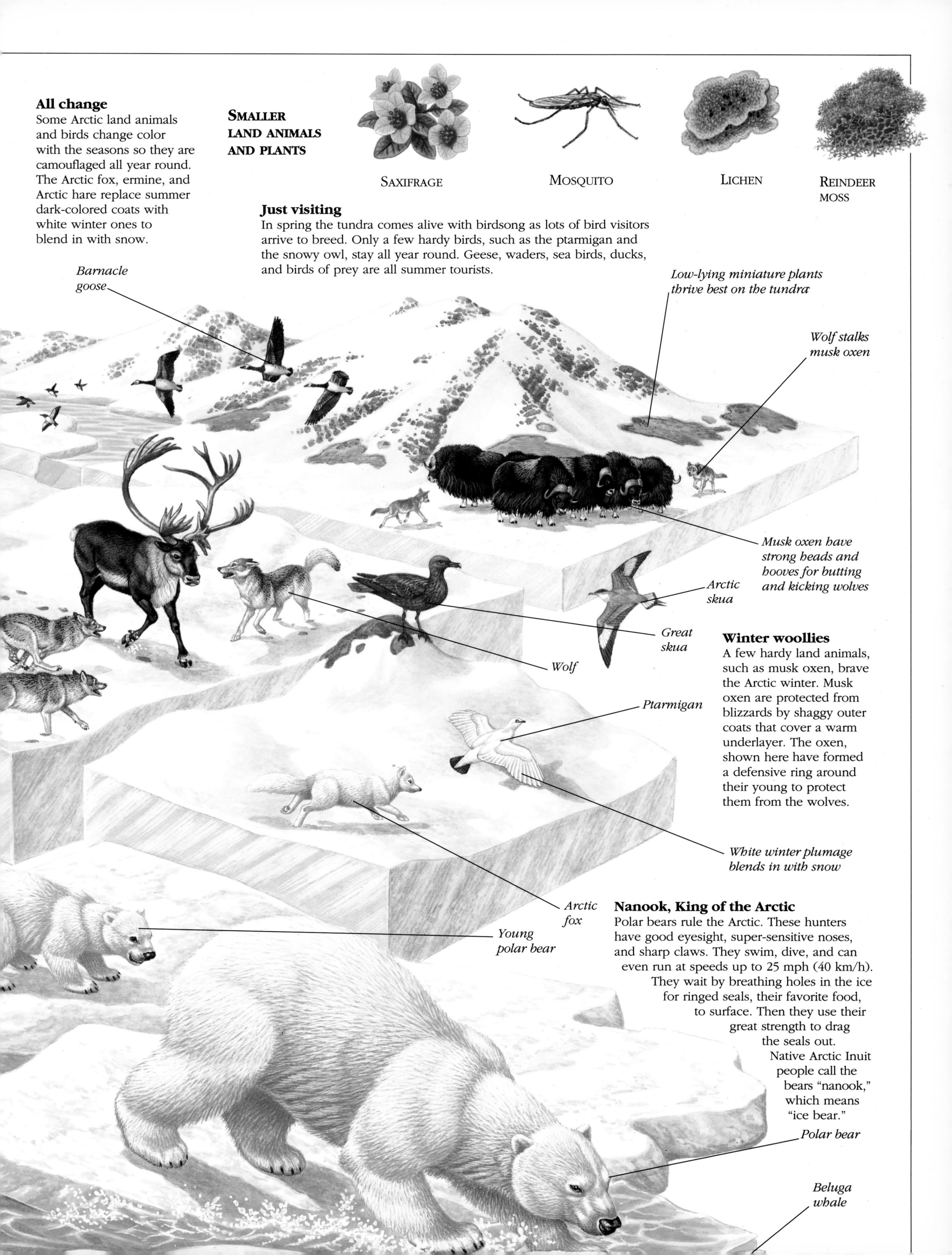

All change
Some Arctic land animals and birds change color with the seasons so they are camouflaged all year round. The Arctic fox, ermine, and Arctic hare replace summer dark-colored coats with white winter ones to blend in with snow.

SMALLER LAND ANIMALS AND PLANTS

SAXIFRAGE

MOSQUITO

LICHEN

REINDEER MOSS

Just visiting
In spring the tundra comes alive with birdsong as lots of bird visitors arrive to breed. Only a few hardy birds, such as the ptarmigan and the snowy owl, stay all year round. Geese, waders, sea birds, ducks, and birds of prey are all summer tourists.

Barnacle goose

Low-lying miniature plants thrive best on the tundra

Wolf stalks musk oxen

Musk oxen have strong heads and hooves for butting and kicking wolves

Arctic skua

Great skua

Wolf

Winter woollies
A few hardy land animals, such as musk oxen, brave the Arctic winter. Musk oxen are protected from blizzards by shaggy outer coats that cover a warm underlayer. The oxen, shown here have formed a defensive ring around their young to protect them from the wolves.

Ptarmigan

White winter plumage blends in with snow

Arctic fox

Young polar bear

Nanook, King of the Arctic
Polar bears rule the Arctic. These hunters have good eyesight, super-sensitive noses, and sharp claws. They swim, dive, and can even run at speeds up to 25 mph (40 km/h). They wait by breathing holes in the ice for ringed seals, their favorite food, to surface. Then they use their great strength to drag the seals out.
Native Arctic Inuit people call the bears "nanook," which means "ice bear."

Polar bear

Beluga whale

White-headed petrel

Great-winged petrel

Cape pigeon

White-chinned petrel

Blue petrel

Young Ross seal

Killer gangs

There are two groups of whales in the Antarctic Ocean. Baleen whales eat krill, sifting it through bony plates in their mouths. Toothed whales hunt for larger prey. Among this group are the fast and ferocious killer whales. They hunt in gangs called pods, working cleverly together to trap seals and other small whales. They have even been known to chase human explorers.

King penguin

Killer whale

Blue-eyed shag

Ross seal

Adelie penguin

Emperor penguin and chick

Adelie penguins

Adelies are the most common Antarctic penguins. They breed in large colonies and, like other penguins, one parent stays sitting on the egg while the other goes to the ocean to feed. When the chicks are three weeks old, they waddle over to join nearby "creches," or huddles of other chicks. These babies stay together to keep warm and safe while both parents go off to find food. When a parent returns, it can recognize its own chick's call.

Emperor penguins

Emperor penguins breed at a different time from all the other Antarctic animals. Each female lays one egg in the fall. She transfers it to the male, who keeps it warm in a pouch above his feet. The males gather together in a huddle while the females go off to the ocean to feed. During this time, the males stand in darkness, without food, enduring the fiercest, coldest winter storms anywhere in the world.

ANTARCTIC LIFE

ANTARCTICA IS A HUGE CONTINENT THE SIZE OF THE US and South America combined. It is the southernmost land on Earth – a barren, dangerous world permanently covered by thick ice and surrounded by the stormy Antarctic Ocean. It lies in darkness for six months of the year and during these bleak winter months, half of the ocean freezes over and temperatures on the mainland fall to -94° F (-70° C). In this climate very few animals can survive, but when the sun returns in September, the ocean begins to melt around the edges of the land. Lots of animals arrive to breed on the shores before the harsh snowstorms of winter return in February.

Gentoo penguin

Elephant seal

Flabby fighters
During the summer, more than 300,000 elephant seals arrive to breed on the Antarctic island of South Georgia. The crowded beaches become noisy, dangerous places as the giant males rear up to fight each other for females. They roar out challenges and crash into each other, biting ferociously.

Antarctic skua

Colonies and crabeaters
Many millions of seals breed in groups called colonies around the edge of Antarctica. Species include Weddell seals, Ross seals, and crabeater seals. There are thought to be as many as thirty million crabeaters, making them by far the largest group. They spend most of their lives in the water or hauled up on floating ice blocks called floes. They look clumsy on land, but in the water they are graceful, acrobatic swimmers.

Crabeater seal

Chinstrap penguin

Baby stealers
Skuas are large seabirds with sharp, hooked beaks. They nest near penguin colonies so they can steal chicks and eggs to eat. They even attack small birds in the air, carrying on daring acrobatic chases until they force their victims to regurgitate the food they have eaten. Small petrels travel to and from their nests under cover of darkness to avoid these vicious airborne pirates.

Dove prion

Ice fish

Antifreeze fish
In winter, when the sea surface has turned to ice, life continues in the icy waters below. Antarctic fish have adapted to survive the cold – most of them have a kind of antifreeze in their bodies that keeps their blood from freezing up.

Snow petrel

Antarctic cod

Toothfish

Krill

Sinister smilers
Leopard seals are well named – just like leopards, they are cunning predators. Along with krill and fish, they like to eat penguins, and even human divers are not safe from their attack. Their upturned mouths give them a sinister-looking smile, concealing ferocious teeth. They will sometimes smash up through a layer of ice to snatch an unsuspecting penguin walking above.

Leopard seal

Counting krill
Krill are small shrimplike creatures about 2 in (5 cm) long. There are an estimated 590 million tons (600 million tonnes) of them altogether. Krill are vital for the survival of the animals that visit Antarctica to breed. In winter they settle underneath the pack ice to eat algae. In summer they swim together in giant swarms, providing a feast for whales, seals, and penguins.

ARCTIC LIFE

MAPMAKERS DRAW AN IMAGINARY LINE, THE ARCTIC CIRCLE, AROUND the top of the world. Inside the circle, the northernmost lands of the Earth surround the Arctic Ocean. The area is so cold that much of it is frozen into a huge sheet of ice. Winter lasts for many months, and it is a time of fierce blizzards, bitingly cold temperatures, and constant darkness. Some animals weather the winter through, but many more arrive in the Arctic's brief summer season. For three or four months the sun shines, and its rays melt some of the ice and snow that cover the land and sea. The animals breed on the tundra, the area of land exposed by the thaw.

Back to breed
Most Arctic animals are summer visitors, and spend the winter farther south. These include herds of caribou many thousands strong that trek up to summer breeding grounds over routes used by their ancestors for centuries. These herds are usually followed by packs of wolves hoping to kill and eat young or sick herd members.

Lemming larder
The lemming is a small but important tundra animal, the main food of many larger creatures. In winter these rodents stay underground; in summer they venture above.

Frozen forever
In spring and summer the tundra is boggy and wet, with tiny flowers and mosses growing on it. But only a little way beneath the surface there is a permanently frozen layer of earth called permafrost.

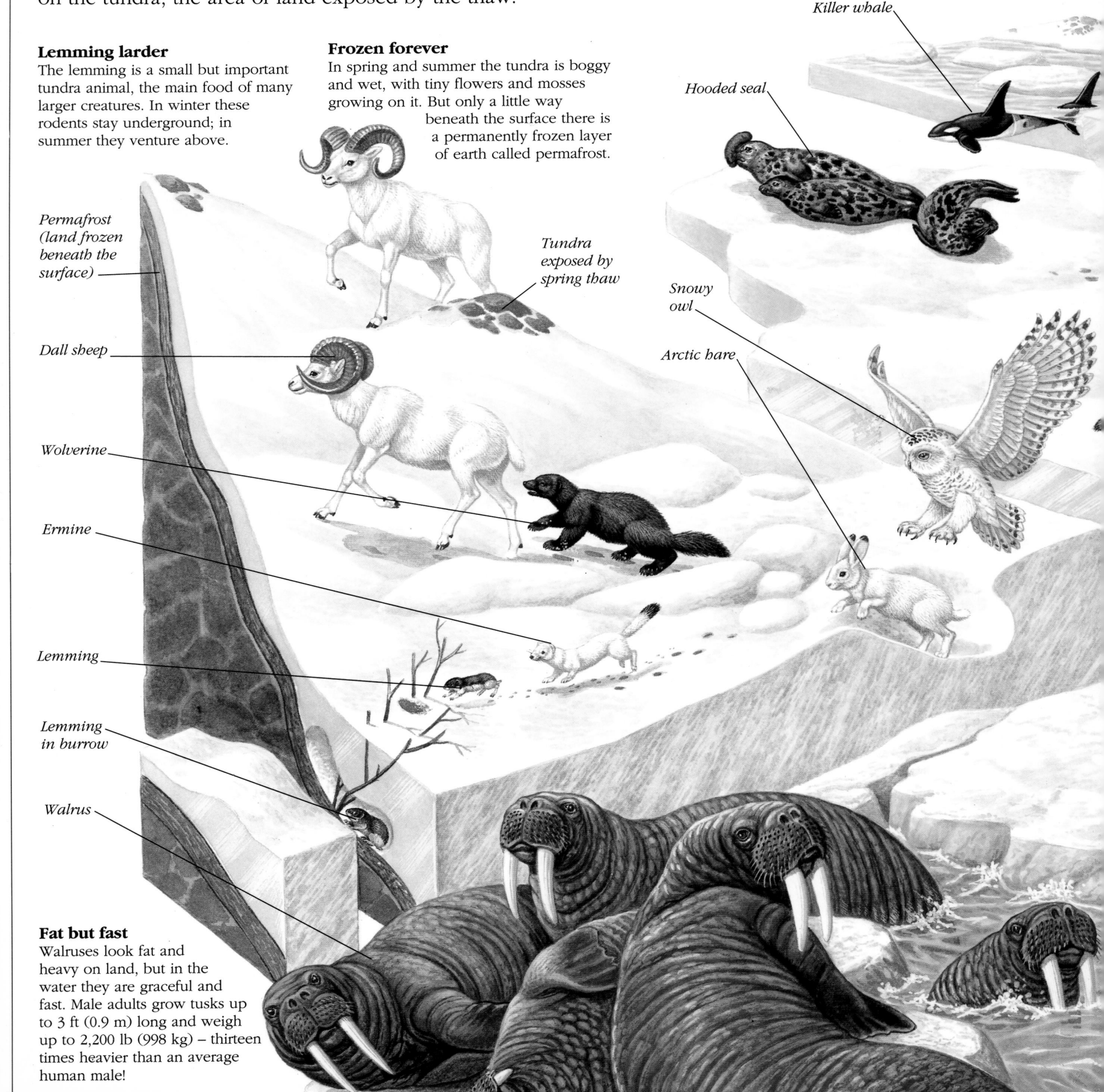

Killer whale

Hooded seal

Permafrost (land frozen beneath the surface)

Dall sheep

Tundra exposed by spring thaw

Snowy owl

Arctic hare

Wolverine

Ermine

Lemming

Lemming in burrow

Walrus

Fat but fast
Walruses look fat and heavy on land, but in the water they are graceful and fast. Male adults grow tusks up to 3 ft (0.9 m) long and weigh up to 2,200 lb (998 kg) – thirteen times heavier than an average human male!

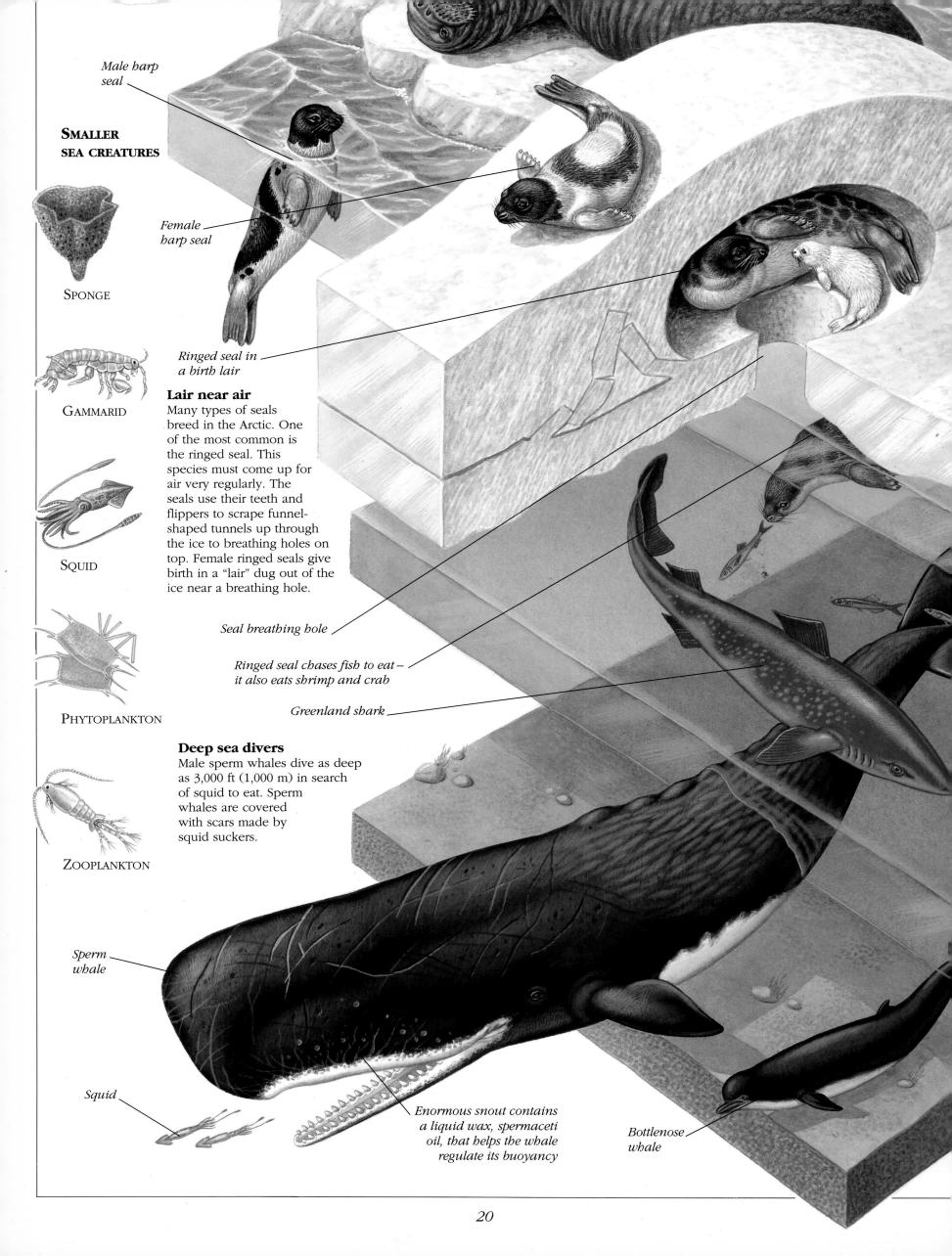

SMALLER SEA CREATURES

SPONGE

GAMMARID

SQUID

PHYTOPLANKTON

ZOOPLANKTON

Male harp seal

Female harp seal

Ringed seal in a birth lair

Lair near air
Many types of seals breed in the Arctic. One of the most common is the ringed seal. This species must come up for air very regularly. The seals use their teeth and flippers to scrape funnel-shaped tunnels up through the ice to breathing holes on top. Female ringed seals give birth in a "lair" dug out of the ice near a breathing hole.

Seal breathing hole

Ringed seal chases fish to eat – it also eats shrimp and crab

Greenland shark

Deep sea divers
Male sperm whales dive as deep as 3,000 ft (1,000 m) in search of squid to eat. Sperm whales are covered with scars made by squid suckers.

Sperm whale

Squid

Enormous snout contains a liquid wax, spermaceti oil, that helps the whale regulate its buoyancy

Bottlenose whale

Tawny owl

Oak bark beetle

All about bark

The bark is the rough outer layer of a tree. It helps prevent damage from animals, stops the tree from drying out, and protects it from heat and cold. As the tree grows thicker, its bark stretches and splits.

Gallery made by oak bark beetle

From the acorn

Acorns are the fruit of the oak tree. Each acorn grows in a cup attached to a twig. The hard acorn shell protects the soft seed inside. Only one in a million acorns makes it to the tree stage. The rest are eaten by animals such as insects, squirrels, and jays. In the Middle Ages, farmers took their pigs into the forest to graze on fallen acorns.

Wood pigeons and nest

Great spotted woodpecker

Stag beetle

Nuthatch

Starling

Wood warbler

Purple emperor

Polecat

Common shrew

Acorn

BIRTH OF A TREE

Sulfur tuft fungi

Garlic snail

Slug

Stag beetle larva

Blusher

Lynx

Song thrush

Gray squirrel

Yellow-necked field mouse

Dryad's saddle

Spindleshank fungus

Mole

Root gall

Rooting around

In spring and summer, the roots suck up water and minerals to help produce the tree's food. In fall and winter, any unused food is carried back down to the roots to be stored underground until the spring. The roots also support the tree; oak roots are particularly strong, so oaks withstand centuries of storms and high winds.

Tree killers

Fungi are plants, but they do not contain chlorophyll and so cannot make food by photosynthesis. They take their food from decaying or living things, including oaks. Spindleshank fungus, shown above, anchors itself to an oak's trunk. Fungi are spread by tiny seeds called spores.

Birth of a tree

Stage 1:
In spring, the seed inside a fallen acorn sends a root down into the soil. The root sucks up water and minerals. **Stage 2:** The seed sends up a shoot into the light and two rounded seed leaves open out to reveal a tiny bud. **Stage 3:** As the first proper tree leaves grow, the leaves lengthen to find more nutrients. In autumn, the leaves fall, leaving a new bud that will start to grow in the spring.

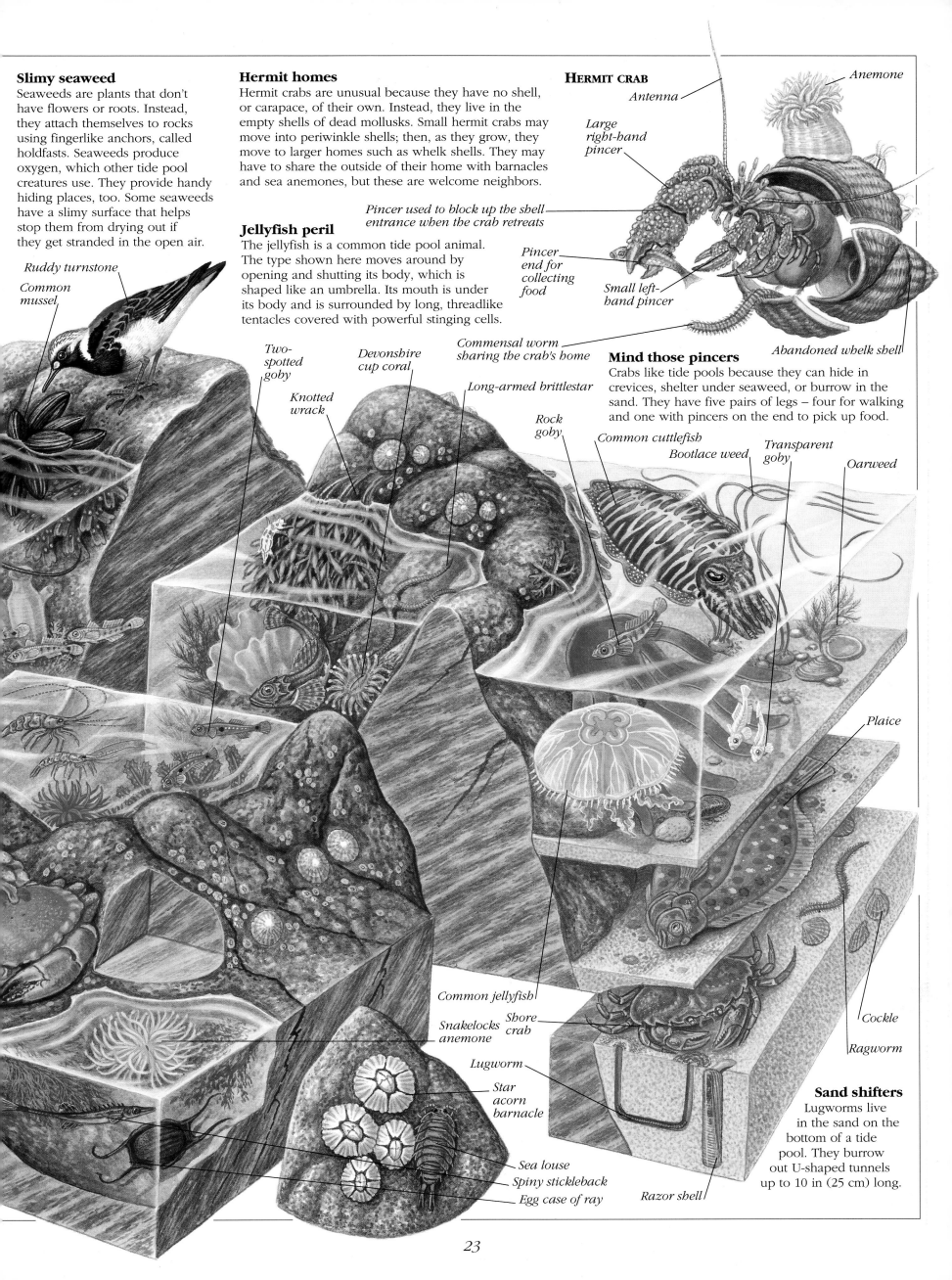

Slimy seaweed

Seaweeds are plants that don't have flowers or roots. Instead, they attach themselves to rocks using fingerlike anchors, called holdfasts. Seaweeds produce oxygen, which other tide pool creatures use. They provide handy hiding places, too. Some seaweeds have a slimy surface that helps stop them from drying out if they get stranded in the open air.

Ruddy turnstone

Common mussel

Hermit homes

Hermit crabs are unusual because they have no shell, or carapace, of their own. Instead, they live in the empty shells of dead mollusks. Small hermit crabs may move into periwinkle shells; then, as they grow, they move to larger homes such as whelk shells. They may have to share the outside of their home with barnacles and sea anemones, but these are welcome neighbors.

Jellyfish peril

The jellyfish is a common tide pool animal. The type shown here moves around by opening and shutting its body, which is shaped like an umbrella. Its mouth is under its body and is surrounded by long, threadlike tentacles covered with powerful stinging cells.

HERMIT CRAB

Antenna

Anemone

Large right-hand pincer

Pincer used to block up the shell entrance when the crab retreats

Pincer end for collecting food

Small left-hand pincer

Commensal worm sharing the crab's home

Abandoned whelk shell

Mind those pincers

Crabs like tide pools because they can hide in crevices, shelter under seaweed, or burrow in the sand. They have five pairs of legs – four for walking and one with pincers on the end to pick up food.

Two-spotted goby

Devonshire cup coral

Knotted wrack

Long-armed brittlestar

Rock goby

Common cuttlefish

Bootlace weed

Transparent goby

Oarweed

Plaice

Common jellyfish

Snakelocks anemone

Shore crab

Lugworm

Star acorn barnacle

Sea louse

Spiny stickleback

Egg case of ray

Cockle

Ragworm

Razor shell

Sand shifters

Lugworms live in the sand on the bottom of a tide pool. They burrow out U-shaped tunnels up to 10 in (25 cm) long.

BEEHIVE

ON A WARM SUMMER DAY YOU MIGHT WELL SEE A BUSY honeybee collecting nectar and flower pollen to take back to its hive. Some of this will be eaten and some of it will be made into delicious honey and be stored in honeycombs to eat during the cold winter months. Honeycombs are six-sided cells, built from wax made inside a bee's body, where the bees bring up infants and store all their food. The wild honeybees in this picture have built their hive in a hollow tree trunk. Inside there are likely to be tens of thousands of bees, but they all work as one highly efficient team. There are three bee "ranks" – the queen, the workers, and the drones.

Bee dancing

When a worker bee finds a good source of nectar or pollen, it comes back to its hive and tells its colleagues. It does this by dancing in a special pattern that communicates the direction and distance of the food. It also brings back a sample for the other bees to try.

Bee babies

The cells in which infants are raised are called brood cells. The queen lays an egg in each one. The eggs hatch into white grubs called larvae and are fed by worker bees. The food they get and the size of their cell determines what rank of bee they will become.

Amazing jelly

Worker bees produce a rich creamy substance called Royal Jelly, which they feed queen larvae. Worker and drone larvae eat a little bit of the jelly, but get more nectar and pollen. After a while the brood cells are covered over with wax and the larvae develop into adults that bite their way out.

WORKER BEE GATHERING NECTAR

Straight stinger

Abdomen

Pollen stored in leg sac

Brushes for moving the pollen off the bee's body into the leg sacs

Tongue

Busy bees

Most bees in a colony are workers. They are females, but they don't lay eggs. They live for about five weeks and during that time they do all the work of looking after the nest. Their jobs include feeding the infants, making wax and building the honeycomb, collecting pollen and nectar, and making honey.

Cell is varnished with propolis, an antiseptic glue made from plant resin

New adult bee emerging

Antennae

Large many-sided "compound" eyes

Worker bee cells measure about 0.19 in (5 mm) across

Larvae in uncapped brood cells

Worker bee flies out to find food

Eggs about 0.07 in (1.88 mm) long, 0.01 in (0.4 mm) wide

Pollen stored in cells

Bee dancing

Honey stored in cells

Worker bee acts as guard

Worker bee collects pollen and nectar

Nectar is carried home in a "honey stomach"

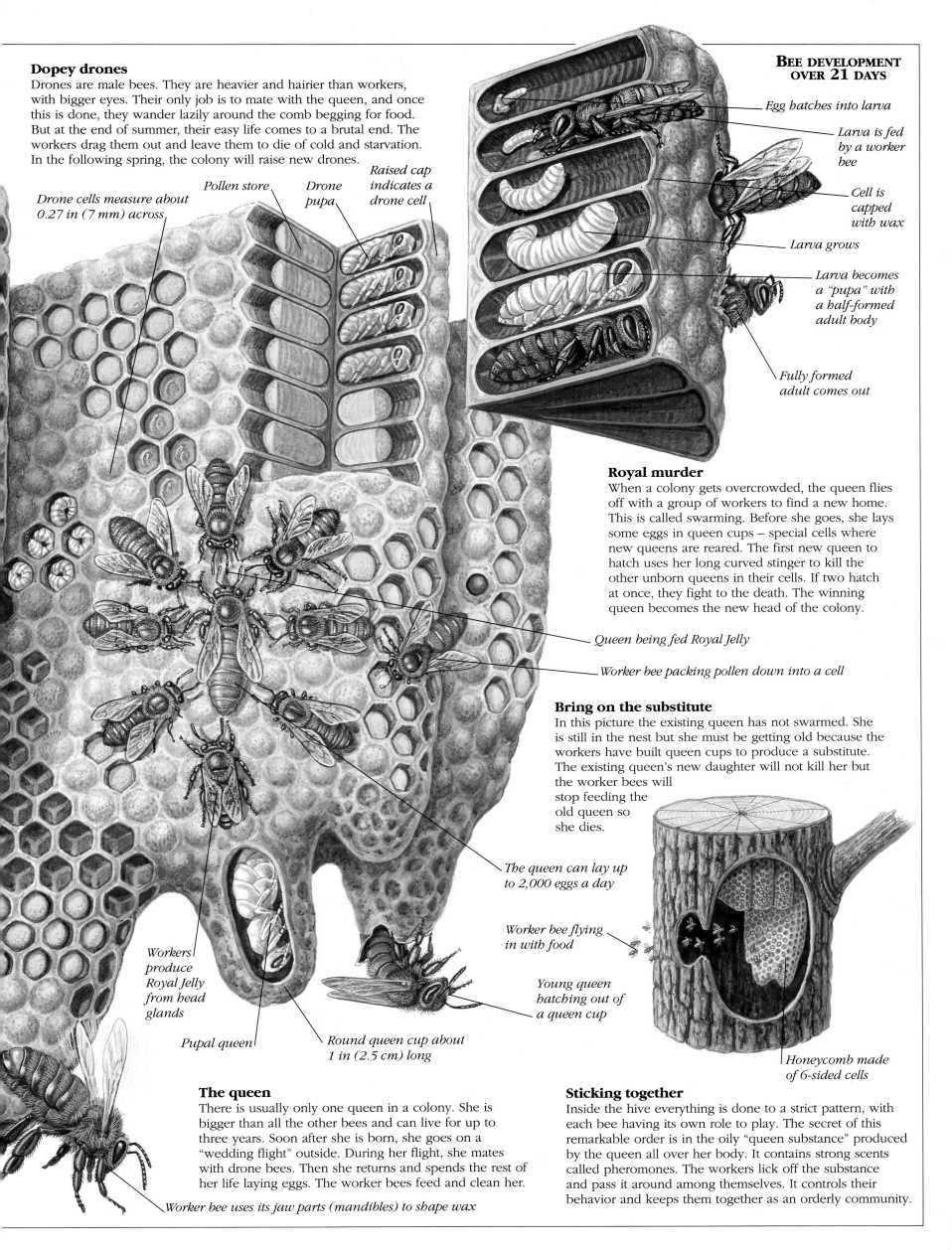

Dopey drones

Drones are male bees. They are heavier and hairier than workers, with bigger eyes. Their only job is to mate with the queen, and once this is done, they wander lazily around the comb begging for food. But at the end of summer, their easy life comes to a brutal end. The workers drag them out and leave them to die of cold and starvation. In the following spring, the colony will raise new drones.

Drone cells measure about 0.27 in (7 mm) across

Pollen store

Drone pupa

Raised cap indicates a drone cell

Egg hatches into larva

Larva is fed by a worker bee

Cell is capped with wax

Larva grows

Larva becomes a "pupa" with a half-formed adult body

Fully formed adult comes out

Royal murder

When a colony gets overcrowded, the queen flies off with a group of workers to find a new home. This is called swarming. Before she goes, she lays some eggs in queen cups – special cells where new queens are reared. The first new queen to hatch uses her long curved stinger to kill the other unborn queens in their cells. If two hatch at once, they fight to the death. The winning queen becomes the new head of the colony.

Queen being fed Royal Jelly

Worker bee packing pollen down into a cell

Bring on the substitute

In this picture the existing queen has not swarmed. She is still in the nest but she must be getting old because the workers have built queen cups to produce a substitute. The existing queen's new daughter will not kill her but the worker bees will stop feeding the old queen so she dies.

The queen can lay up to 2,000 eggs a day

Worker bee flying in with food

Young queen hatching out of a queen cup

Honeycomb made of 6-sided cells

Workers produce Royal Jelly from head glands

Pupal queen

Round queen cup about 1 in (2.5 cm) long

The queen

There is usually only one queen in a colony. She is bigger than all the other bees and can live for up to three years. Soon after she is born, she goes on a "wedding flight" outside. During her flight, she mates with drone bees. Then she returns and spends the rest of her life laying eggs. The worker bees feed and clean her.

Worker bee uses its jaw parts (mandibles) to shape wax

Sticking together

Inside the hive everything is done to a strict pattern, with each bee having its own role to play. The secret of this remarkable order is in the oily "queen substance" produced by the queen all over her body. It contains strong scents called pheromones. The workers lick off the substance and pass it around among themselves. It controls their behavior and keeps them together as an orderly community.

AMERICAN DESERT

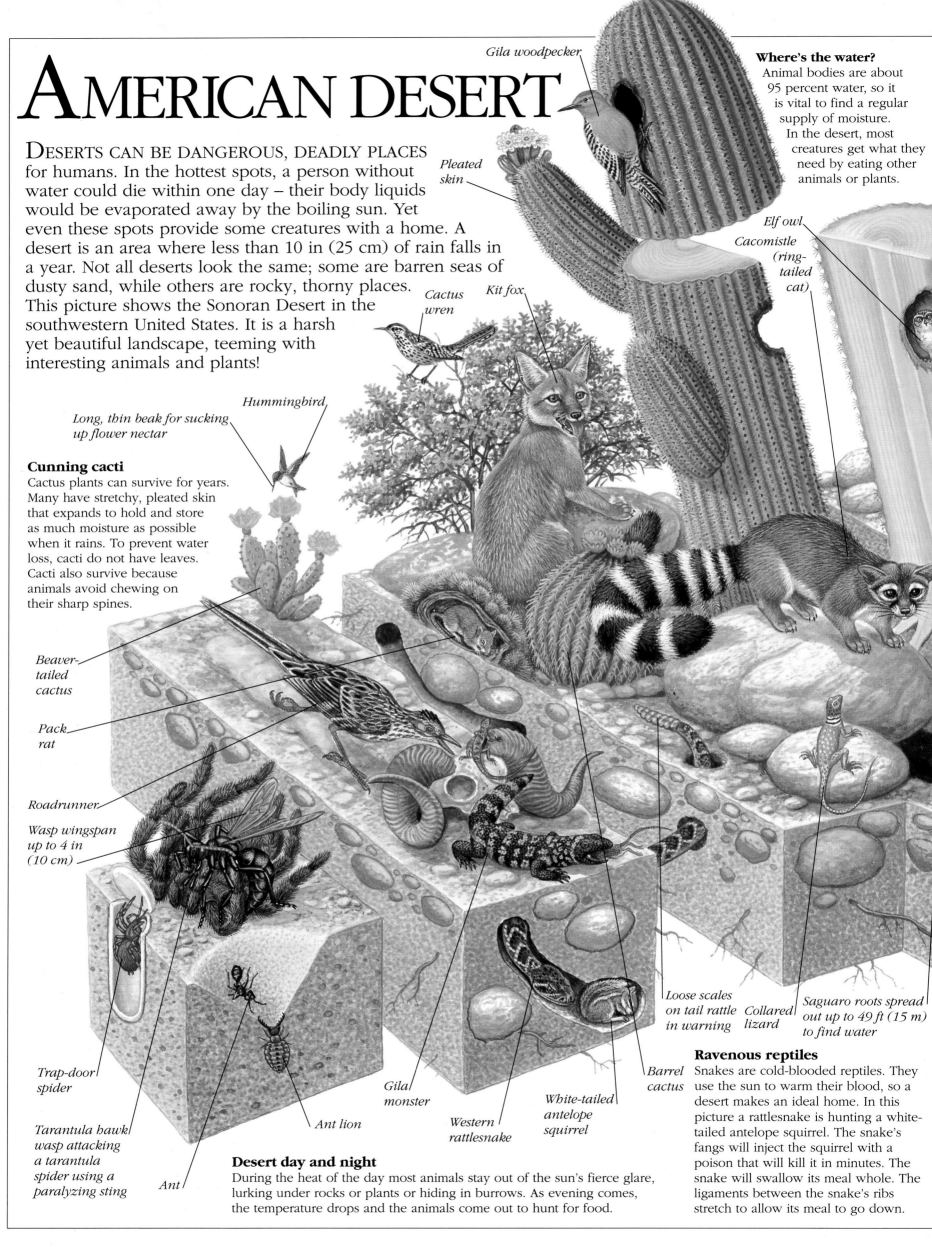

DESERTS CAN BE DANGEROUS, DEADLY PLACES for humans. In the hottest spots, a person without water could die within one day – their body liquids would be evaporated away by the boiling sun. Yet even these spots provide some creatures with a home. A desert is an area where less than 10 in (25 cm) of rain falls in a year. Not all deserts look the same; some are barren seas of dusty sand, while others are rocky, thorny places. This picture shows the Sonoran Desert in the southwestern United States. It is a harsh yet beautiful landscape, teeming with interesting animals and plants!

Where's the water?
Animal bodies are about 95 percent water, so it is vital to find a regular supply of moisture. In the desert, most creatures get what they need by eating other animals or plants.

Gila woodpecker

Pleated skin

Elf owl

Cacomistle (ring-tailed cat)

Cactus wren

Kit fox

Hummingbird

Long, thin beak for sucking up flower nectar

Cunning cacti
Cactus plants can survive for years. Many have stretchy, pleated skin that expands to hold and store as much moisture as possible when it rains. To prevent water loss, cacti do not have leaves. Cacti also survive because animals avoid chewing on their sharp spines.

Beaver-tailed cactus

Pack rat

Roadrunner

Wasp wingspan up to 4 in (10 cm)

Trap-door spider

Tarantula hawk wasp attacking a tarantula spider using a paralyzing sting

Ant

Ant lion

Gila monster

Western rattlesnake

White-tailed antelope squirrel

Loose scales on tail rattle in warning

Collared lizard

Saguaro roots spread out up to 49 ft (15 m) to find water

Barrel cactus

Desert day and night
During the heat of the day most animals stay out of the sun's fierce glare, lurking under rocks or plants or hiding in burrows. As evening comes, the temperature drops and the animals come out to hunt for food.

Ravenous reptiles
Snakes are cold-blooded reptiles. They use the sun to warm their blood, so a desert makes an ideal home. In this picture a rattlesnake is hunting a white-tailed antelope squirrel. The snake's fangs will inject the squirrel with a poison that will kill it in minutes. The snake will swallow its meal whole. The ligaments between the snake's ribs stretch to allow its meal to go down.

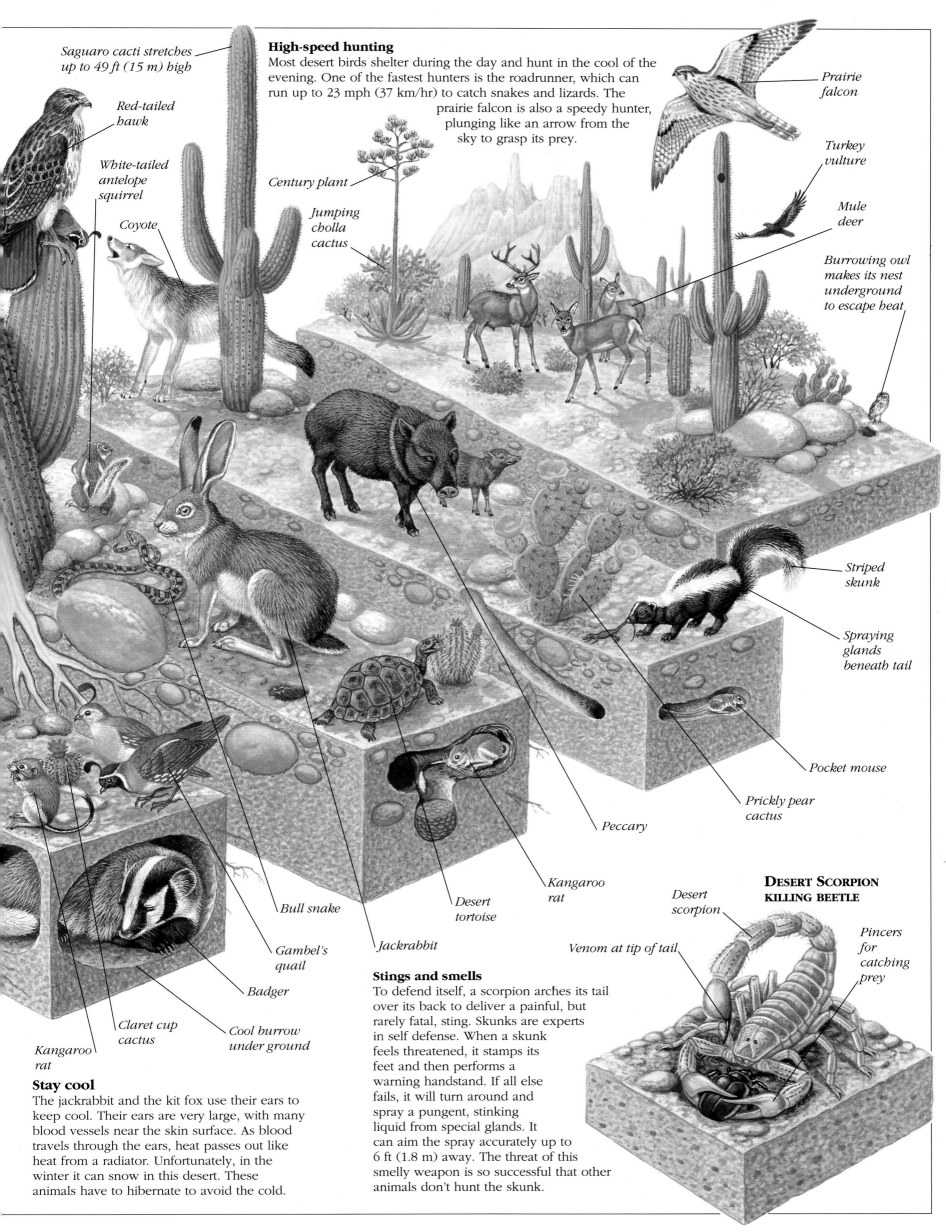

Saguaro cacti stretches up to 49 ft (15 m) high

Red-tailed hawk

White-tailed antelope squirrel

Coyote

High-speed hunting
Most desert birds shelter during the day and hunt in the cool of the evening. One of the fastest hunters is the roadrunner, which can run up to 23 mph (37 km/hr) to catch snakes and lizards. The prairie falcon is also a speedy hunter, plunging like an arrow from the sky to grasp its prey.

Century plant

Jumping cholla cactus

Prairie falcon

Turkey vulture

Mule deer

Burrowing owl makes its nest underground to escape heat

Striped skunk

Spraying glands beneath tail

Pocket mouse

Prickly pear cactus

Peccary

Kangaroo rat

Desert tortoise

Jackrabbit

Bull snake

Gambel's quail

Badger

Claret cup cactus

Cool burrow under ground

Kangaroo rat

DESERT SCORPION
KILLING BEETLE

Desert scorpion

Venom at tip of tail

Pincers for catching prey

Stings and smells
To defend itself, a scorpion arches its tail over its back to deliver a painful, but rarely fatal, sting. Skunks are experts in self defense. When a skunk feels threatened, it stamps its feet and then performs a warning handstand. If all else fails, it will turn around and spray a pungent, stinking liquid from special glands. It can aim the spray accurately up to 6 ft (1.8 m) away. The threat of this smelly weapon is so successful that other animals don't hunt the skunk.

Stay cool
The jackrabbit and the kit fox use their ears to keep cool. Their ears are very large, with many blood vessels near the skin surface. As blood travels through the ears, heat passes out like heat from a radiator. Unfortunately, in the winter it can snow in this desert. These animals have to hibernate to avoid the cold.

OCEAN

PHOTOGRAPHS OF THE EARTH TAKEN FROM OUTER SPACE LOOK MOSTLY blue. About 70 percent of the Earth's surface is covered by ocean, so the blue color is the water. If you dove beneath the waves, you would find an amazing watery world where creatures of all shapes and sizes make their homes, from giant ferocious sharks to tiny floating animals too small for humans to see. Sea life varies depending on the depth and temperature of the water. This picture shows some of the animals to be found in the Pacific Ocean.

Snacks for sea birds
Sea birds gather wherever there is food near the water's surface. Some of them dive for fish; others float on top of the waves spearing fish with their beaks. Some are even pirates, stealing food from other birds. They all have oil-covered feathers that keep them waterproof. Most sea birds live close to the coast, but a few spend many months far out at sea.

You're lunch!
In the sea, tiny fish are eaten by small fish, which are then eaten by large fish. This is known as a food chain. At the beginning of the ocean food chain there are tiny floating plants called phytoplankton, found near the sea's surface. They are eaten by microscopic creatures called zooplankton.

Danger at the top
On the surface floats a Portuguese man o'war. Its poisonous tentacles kill any fish that swims too near.

CROSS-SECTION THROUGH CORAL

All about corals
Corals need warm water and sunlight, so they are found where the seabed is near the surface. Corals are made up of many tiny animals called polyps. Each polyp has a ring of tentacles that it uses to sieve particles of food from the water around it. Some corals are hard and some are soft. Each hard coral polyp grows a limestone case to protect itself.

EPIPELAGIC ZONE

Laysan albatross

Frigate birds

Sailfish

Flying fish

Portuguese man o'war

Hammerhead shark

Powder blue surgeon fish

Common dolphin

Blue angel fish

Blue-footed booby

Ling cod

Barred surf perch

Snapper

Manta ray

Pacific barracuda

Pacific sardine

Eastern little tuna

Spotted moray eel

Sheepshead

Unicorn-fish

Four saddle puffer

Ocean sunfish

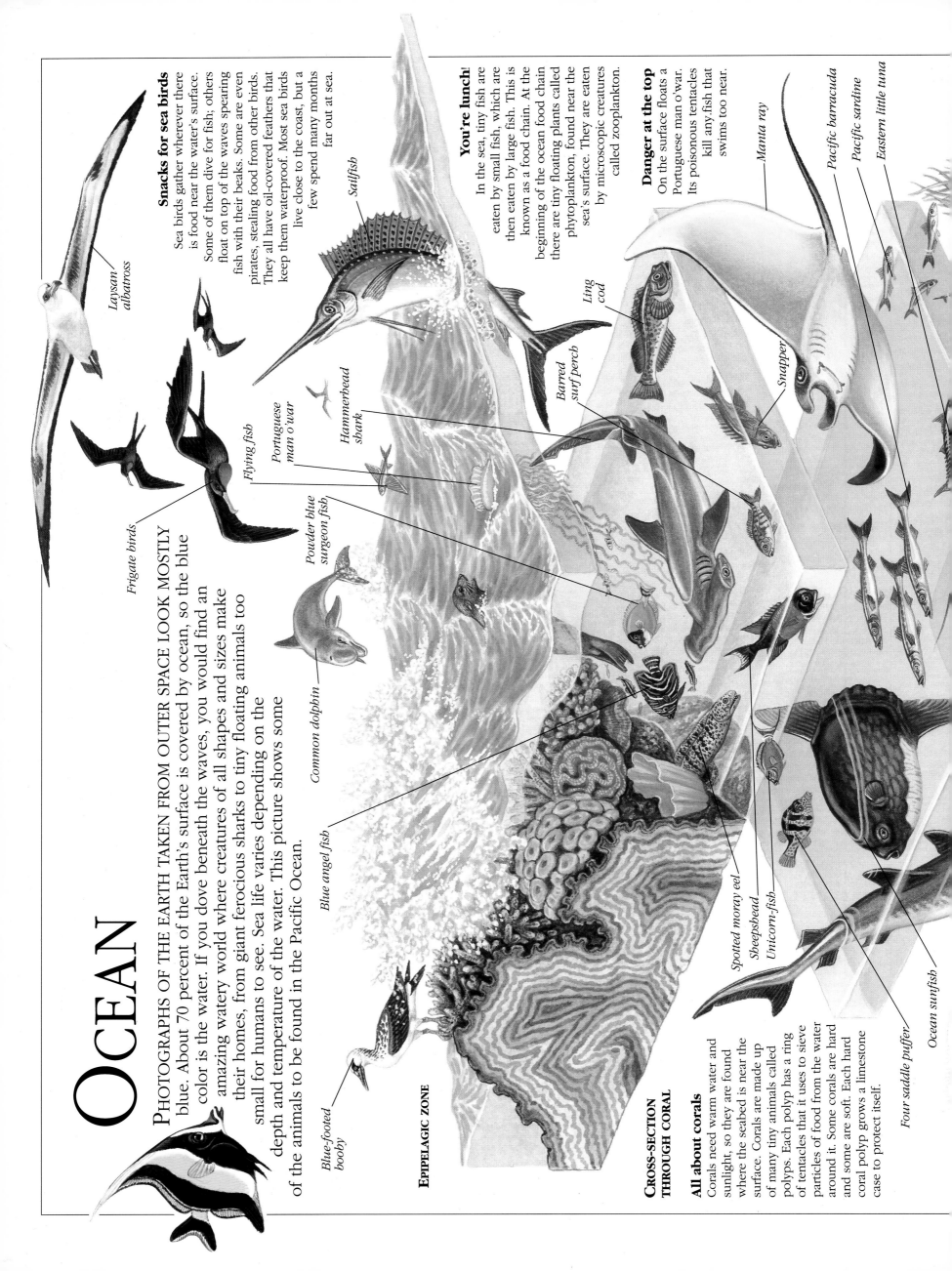

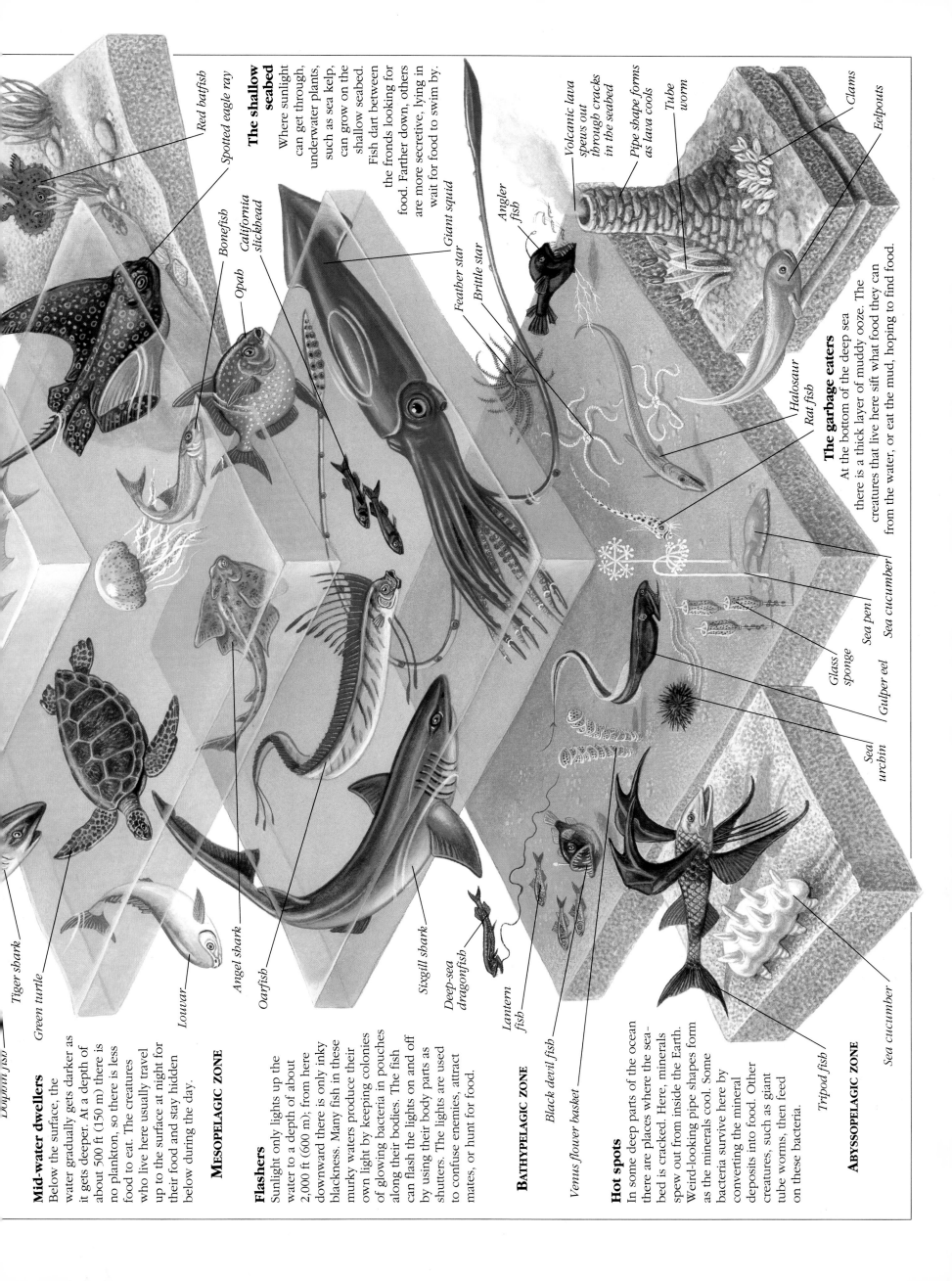

Red batfish

Spotted eagle ray

The shallow seabed
Where sunlight can get through, underwater plants, such as sea kelp, can grow on the shallow seabed. Fish dart between the fronds looking for food, others are more secretive, lying in wait for food to swim by.

Bonefish

Opah

California slickhead

Giant squid

Feather star

Brittle star

Angler fish

Volcanic lava spews out through cracks in the seabed

Pipe shape forms as lava cools

Tube worm

Clams

Eelpouts

Halosaur

Rat fish

Glass sponge

Sea pen

Sea cucumber

Gulper eel

Sea urchin

Tiger shark

Green turtle

Mid-water dwellers
Below the surface, the water gradually gets darker as it gets deeper. At a depth of about 500 ft (150 m) there is no plankton, so there is less food to eat. The creatures who live here usually travel up to the surface at night for their food and stay hidden below during the day.

MESOPELAGIC ZONE

Flashers
Sunlight only lights up the water to a depth of about 2,000 ft (600 m); from here downward there is only inky blackness. Many fish in these murky waters produce their own light by keeping colonies of glowing bacteria in pouches along their bodies. The fish can flash the lights on and off by using their body parts as shutters. The lights are used to confuse enemies, attract mates, or hunt for food.

Louvar

Angel shark

Oarfish

Sixgill shark

Deep-sea dragonfish

Lantern fish

BATHYPELAGIC ZONE

Black devil fish

Venus flower basket

Hot spots
In some deep parts of the ocean there are places where the sea-bed is cracked. Here, minerals spew out from inside the Earth. Weird-looking pipe shapes form as the minerals cool. Some bacteria survive here by converting the mineral deposits into food. Other creatures, such as giant tube worms, then feed on these bacteria.

The garbage eaters
At the bottom of the deep sea there is a thick layer of muddy ooze. The creatures that live here sift what food they can from the water, or eat the mud, hoping to find food.

Tripod fish

ABYSSOPELAGIC ZONE

Sea cucumber

INDEX

ACKNOWLEDGMENTS

Dorling Kindersley would like to thank the following people who helped in the preparation of this book:

Shaila Awan for editorial assistance

Lynn Bresler for the index